BAD HABITS

BY TERRENCE MCNALLY

★

★

DRAMATISTS
PLAY SERVICE
INC.

For Elaine May

BAD HABITS opened February 4, 1974, at the Astor Place Theatre, and then on May 5, 1974, at the Booth Theatre in New York City. It was produced by Adela Holzer. It was directed by Robert Drivas. Scenery and costumes designed by Michael H. Yeargan and Lawrence King. Lighting designed by Ken Billington. The production stage manager was Robert Vandergriff. The assistant to the director and assistant stage manager was Tony DeSantis. The cast was as follows:

For DUNELAWN:

OTTO ....Henry Sutton
APRIL PITT ....Cynthia Harris
ROY PITT ....F. Murray Abraham
JASON PEPPER, M.D. ....Paul Benedict
DOLLY SCUPP..Doris Roberts
HIRAM SPANE ....Emory Bass
FRANCIS TEAR ....J. Frank Lucas
HARRY SCUPP ....Michael Lombard

For RAVENSWOOD:

RUTH BENSON, R.N. ....Cynthia Harris
BECKY HEDGES, R.N. ....Doris Roberts
BRUNO ....Henry Sutton
MR. PONCE ....Emory Bass
DR. TOYNBEE ....J. Frank Lucas
MR. BLUM ....F. Murray Abraham
MR. YAMADORO ....Michael Lombard
HUGH GUMBS ....Paul Benedict

This revised version of BAD HABITS was produced at the Manhattan Theatre Club (Lynne Meadow, Artistic Director; Barry Grove, Managing Director) in New York City on February 27, 1990. It was directed by Paul Benedict; the set design was by John Lee Beatty; lighting design was by Peter Kaczorowski; costume design was by Jane Greenwood; sound design was by John Gromada. The production stage manager was Tom Aberger; the assistant to the director was Dominic Cuskern; the assistant to Mr. McNally was Elyse Singer. The cast was as follows:

For DUNELAWN:

OTTO	Ralph Marrero
APRIL PITT	Kate Nelligan
ROY PITT	Robert Clohessy
JASON PEPPER, M.D.	Nathan Lane
DOLLY SCUPP	Faith Prince
HIRAM SPANE	David Cromwell
FRANCIS TEAR	Bill Buell
HARRY SCUPP	Michael Mantell

For RAVENSWOOD:

RUTH BENSON, R.N.	Kate Nelligan
BECKY HEDGES, R.N.	Faith Prince
BRUNO	Robert Clohessy
MR. PONCE	Bill Buell
DR. TOYNBEE	David Cromwell
MR. BLUM	Michael Mantell
MR. YAMADORO	Ralph Marrero
HUGH GUMBS	Nathan Lane

DUNELAWN

THE PLAYERS

OTTO
APRIL PITT
ROY PITT
JASON PEPPER, M.D.
DOLLY SCUPP
HIRAM SPANE
FRANCIS TEAR
HARRY SCUPP

BAD HABITS

DUNELAWN

Bright sunlight. Lush green foliage. Heaven on earth. Otto is discovered arranging luncheon flowers on the tables that dot the terrace. He is listening to music on a portable cassette player as he works. Edith Piaf singing "Je ne regrette rien" perhaps. From off-stage we hear the sounds of a car driving up the gravel driveway fast, the brakes are slammed on, the engine stops, then car doors opening and slamming.

APRIL. *(Off.)* Hello! We're here!

ROY. *(Off.)* Checking in! Checking in!

APRIL. *(Off.)* Hello, somebody! Yoo hoo!

ROY. *(Off.)* Does somebody want to give us a hand with these things?

APRIL. *(Off.)* Front! Front!

ROY. *(Off.)* Hey, where is everybody? You got a couple of new arrivals out here! *(Otto exits in the direction of their voices. The stage is bare a moment.)*

PUBLIC ADDRESS SYSTEM.   Good morning campers. There will be a semi-staged reading of *Hedda Gabler* in the Greek Amphitheatre immediately after lunch. *(A moment or two later, Roy Pitt bounds onto the terrace. He carries a tennis racket and seems extremely pleased with himself to be there. A few steps behind him is April, his wife, who also carries a tennis racket.)*

APRIL.   So this is Dunelawn!

ROY.   Finally! Pinch yourself, honey, we're really here.

APRIL.   It's nice. Very, very nice. I'm impressed.

ROY.   What do you mean, nice? It's sensational! Look at that clay court, April. Real clay. Can you stand it? I'm a poor kid from the Bronx. I could cry. *(He does. April is dry-eyed. Otto returns carrying too much expensive luggage.)* You need a hand, amigo?

APRIL. *(Under her breath.)* Roy!

ROY. What, pumpkin?

APRIL. They got people for that! Jesus, where do you think we are, the Catskills?

ROY. At least I know better than to stand in a driveway yelling "Front, front!"

APRIL. He came, didn't he? Fuck you!

ROY. Fuck you, too, and we just got here!

APRIL. Not a moment too soon!

ROY. You started it.

APRIL. All I said was "Where do you think we are, the Catskills?"

ROY. I said, fuck you.

APRIL. And I said, fuck you, too. *(Short stand-off. They both seem genuinely miserable. Otto is completely non-plussed as he handles their excess and excessive luggage.)* I'm sorry, Roy.

ROY. Me, too, pussycat.

APRIL. I don't want this.

ROY. You think I do? I love you, April!

APRIL. I love you, too, Roy. *(They kiss and make-up. Pretty soon Roy will be nibbling at her ear and generally making out. Otto starts off with the luggage. Even in the throes of passion, April doesn't miss a thing.)*

APRIL. That's Vuitton, buddy!

OTTO. *Ja, fraulein.*

APRIL. Just thought I'd mention it.

OTTO. *Ja, fraulein. (He is gone.)*

APRIL. Jesus, Roy, it's the Gestapo. *(Roy is still nuzzling her.)*

ROY. As soon as we get to that room, I'm going to tear your clothes off with my teeth and make love to you like a dog. *(April pushes him off.)*

APRIL. Fuck you, Roy.

ROY. What did I say?

APRIL. I mean it this time, too.

ROY. What did I say, for Christ's sake?

APRIL. I'm not a dog.

ROY. Of course you're not a dog! Did I say you were a dog? Did I say she was a dog?

APRIL. You said you were going to make love to me like a dog. And will you keep your voice down!

ROY. I was talking about passion, this great animal passion I feel for my beautiful, sexy, sensational wife.

APRIL. Oh. Well why didn't you say so? *(Roy is all over her again with his hands and mouth. April is melting.)*

ROY. It's called lust, April. Good, old-fashioned l-u-s-t. Dog was just a metaphor for you, honey.

APRIL. For you, too! Don't stop, don't stop!

ROY. Did you bring the clothespins?

APRIL. You are so bad, Roy.

ROY. No, *we* are so bad. Why do you think you married me? She brought the clothespins!

APRIL. I just hope this Pepper fellow's all he's cracked up to be.

ROY. I told you: he's just gonna have us talk to each other.

APRIL. We talk to each other all the time. That's when we get into trouble. What's he gonna do?

ROY. Listen.

APRIL. Just listen? Four hundred and fifty clams a day and he just listens?

ROY. That's including room, meals and unlimited use of the facilities. Night tennis, honey. We can boff our brains out and then play singles.

APRIL. I knew I should have checked this guy out first.

ROY. He did wonders for Sandy and Reg.

APRIL. Sandy and Reg are lesbians and they're not in show business. They run a pet shop in Montauk for Christ's sake!

ROY. But they're happy.

APRIL. Sure, they're in dyke heaven, those two. I'm talking about us, Roy, normal people.

ROY. So am I, April, so am I! The man's a genius. He's been on "Donahue," "Geraldo," "Oprah," "Sixty Minutes," the "Today Show," "Good Morning, America," Good Night, America. Let's face it, the guy has credentials. We're lucky he took us.

APRIL. He's lucky we can afford him.

11

ROY. There you go again!

APRIL. What? Where?

ROY. Subtly putting me down. Like Dunelawn wasn't such a good idea.

APRIL. That's not what I said.

ROY. Look, we don't have our first session with him until after lunch. Try to hold out, will you? I will. 'Cause right now, for example, I want to tear your head off. *(He laughs as he says this.)* But never mind, never mind! We're safe from each other, here at Dunelawn! *(He starts off.)* You told the answering service where we'd be? I don't want to miss that call from the Coast.

APRIL. Call? What call? What Coast?

ROY. There's only one Coast, honey.

APRIL. You're expecting a call from the West Coast? Since when? For what? Talk to me, Roy! *(Roy has started singing.)*

ROY. "When I hear them calling me-ee-ee-ee-ee-ee-ee."

APRIL. I hate you when you get like this, Roy. *(He is gone. April will follow.)* This Pepper fellow is going to have his hands full with you. Next to you I'm *The Song of Bernadette! (She is gone. The stage is bare a moment. We hear the sound of an elephant trumpeting from across the lake.)*

PUBLIC ADDRESS SYSTEM. Sexual Aerobics with Debby is beginning on the South Terrace. Toning Your Inner Thigh With Randy is getting underway in Booth Hall. *(Jason Pepper, M.D., has entered with Dolly Scupp. He is in an electric wheelchair with a blanket over his legs. He is drinking a martini and smoking a cigarette. Dolly's right foot is in an orthopedic foot-covering.)*

DR. PEPPER. Over there's our lake. Duck Lake. Swan sounded pretentious. A pond you might call it, but I like to think of it as a lake. After all, it's the only body of water for miles and miles. In the winter it's frozen over and quite covered with snow. And now look at it. Ah, the seasons, the seasons! I do love the seasons. What would we do without them?

DOLLY. What's that across the lake? It looks like a prison.

DR. PEPPER. Some call it Ravenswood. I call it the Tenth Circle.

DOLLY. So that's Ravenswood.

DR. PEPPER.   Your husband's very lucky you didn't send him there.

DOLLY.   I didn't realize you fronted the same lake.

DR. PEPPER.   Believe me, that's all we have in common.

DOLLY.   You look different on your book jacket.

DR. PEPPER.   I know. Taller. May I? *(Dolly hands him a book she has been carrying under her arm.) Marriage For The Fun Of It!* Don't tell me people are still reading this old thing?

DOLLY.   Everybody who wants to stay married. It's their Bible.

DR. PEPPER.   I thought I knew something in those days.

DOLLY.   You're being modest.

DR. PEPPER.   It's my only virtue. *(There is the rumbling of distant thunder. Dr. Pepper puts both hands to his head and gingerly fingers his skull.)* Don't tell me that's not the music of the spheres. It's a day like this that makes you think the world is coming to an end. Only the real joke is, it's not going to rain. Now don't get me wrong: I don't enjoy playing God *or* the weatherman, but I don't have this porous platinum plate in my head for nothing, either. Harry didn't tell me you were coming.

DOLLY.   He didn't know.

DR. PEPPER.   It's a delightful surprise.

DOLLY.   I hope so. I woke up this morning and said to myself, "Enough's enough. I'm driving up to Dunelawn today and see what's going on." I haven't heard a single word from Harry since he got here. Three months! Not even a phone call.

DR. PEPPER.   I'm glad you came. Your absence has made Harry's rehabilitation somewhat more difficult, you understand. I prefer to treat couples who are having difficulties *as* couples.

DOLLY.   There's nothing wrong with me, if that's what you're getting at.

DR. PEPPER.   Should I be?

DOLLY.   I just want to know: is my husband getting any better, Dr. Pepper?

DR. PEPPER.   It's Jason, please, Mrs. Scupp. I insist on it.

13

Until we're over that little hurdle, we're nowhere. Coffee?

DOLLY.   Is it de-caf?

DR. PEPPER.   Good Lord, I hope not.

DOLLY.   I only drink de-caf.

DR. PEPPER.   I'd hate to be your lower intestine.

DOLLY.   Even water de-caffeinated Colombian—?

DR. PEPPER.   *Especially* water de-caffeinated Colombian. Cigarette?

DOLLY.   No, thank you.

DR. PEPPER.   It's a special organic tobacco from Panama that's been fertilized with hen feces. The taste is extraordinarily ... what's the word I'm looking for?

DOLLY.   Shitty! *(She laughs, then recovers.)* I'm sorry. *(She's not, really.)*

DR. PEPPER.   ...*Pungent!* You don't know what you're missing.

DOLLY.   I don't smoke.

DR. PEPPER.   *Et tu, Brute?*

DOLLY.   I gave them up years ago.

DR. PEPPER.   During the Big Scare, hunh? So many of you poor bastards did. *(He is lighting up.)*

DOLLY.   My doctor insisted.

DR. PEPPER.   And who might that be?

DOLLY.   Dr. Fernald.

DR. PEPPER.   Helmut Fernald up at Grassyview? I might've known he'd jump on the bandwagon.

DOLLY.   No, Dr. George Fernald in White Plains, the County Medical Center.

DR. PEPPER.   George Fernald? He wouldn't drive a white Mercedes station wagon, usually there's a couple of dalmations yapping around in the back, I think he breeds them in his off-hours, and be married to one of the Vanderbilts, would he?

DOLLY.   I'm afraid not. Our Dr. Fernald's married to a Korean girl and I'm pretty sure they have a dachshund. I don't know what he drives. He's just our family doctor.

DR. PEPPER.   Well that explains it. The bane of modern medicine, that lot.

DOLLY.   Dr. Fernald?

DR. PEPPER.   No, your friendly, neighborhood family G.P.

14

You don't want to get me started on *them*, Mrs. Scupp.

DOLLY.   I'm sorry but I thought the majority of doctors had stopped smoking, too.

DR. PEPPER.   And doesn't that just sound like something the majority of doctors would do? The Lemming Principle! But fortunately there remain a few of us who refuse to be stampeded along with the common herd. I'm referring to the giants in our industry, of course. Men like Peabody Fowler of the Hetzel Foundation and Otis Strunk of the Merton Institute. *(Dolly shakes her head.)* Rand Baskerville out at Las Palmetas? Mercy! Claude Kitteridge up at Nag's Head. His work with radiated Doberman pinschers is breathtaking.

DOLLY.   I'm sorry.

DR. PEPPER.   I'm speechless.

DOLLY.   I'm just not familiar with them.

DR. PEPPER.   Who is? *(He howls to the heavens.)* I can't discuss colors with a blind person, Mrs. Scupp.

DOLLY.   But seriously, Doctor, you're not suggesting that smoking is good for you?

DR. PEPPER.   Don't be ridiculous. What I am suggesting— and now see if you can follow this — is that not smoking is conceivably worse.

DOLLY.   I don't understand—!

DR. PEPPER.   Do you want to talk turkey or not, Mrs. Scupp?

DOLLY.   Of course I do! What do you think I'm doing here? And please, doctor, call me Dolly.

DR. PEPPER.   Hello, Dolly.

DOLLY.   Hello.

DR. PEPPER.   Well hello, Dolly. There! It's out of my system.

DOLLY.   It's my curse.

DR. PEPPER.   You think Dr. Pepper is easy? Now, I'll start at the beginning and I'll try to keep it in layperson's terms.

DOLLY.   Thank you.

DR. PEPPER.   Everything in life is bad for you.

DOLLY.   You can say that again.

DR. PEPPER.   Everything in life is bad for you. The air we breathe, the sun we live under, the water we drink, the force of gravity, butter, eggs, Haagen-Dazs Macadamia Brittle, the entire Pepperidge Farm American Collection, really good looking shoes, Andrew Lloyd Webber musicals, peanut butter.

DOLLY. Don't tell me they've started in on peanut butter!

DR. PEPPER. There's an article on Peter Pan Extra Crunchy in this month's *The Well Tempered Pancreas* that will stand your hair on end.

DOLLY. Where will it all end, doctor?

DR. PEPPER. Right now, as I speak these very words, you are ten seconds closer to death than when I began them. Eleven seconds, twelve seconds, thirteen. Have I made my point?

DOLLY. I am suddenly so depressed.

DR. PEPPER. Now how would an ice-cold, extra-dry, straight-up Beefeater's gin martini grab you? *(He rings a service bell.)*

DOLLY. I'm afraid it wouldn't.

DR. PEPPER. Ah, vodka is the lovely lady from Scarsdale's poison.

DOLLY. I'm on the wagon.

DR. PEPPER. You don't smoke, you don't drink....

DOLLY. And it's Larchmont. We make our home in Larchmont. And I would like to talk about my husband. *(Otto appears.)*

OTTO. Ze newlyweds have arrived.

DR. PEPPER. Ze newlyweds Pitt?

OTTO. *Ja, Herr Doktor.* I put zem in ze little honeymoon cabin.

DR. PEPPER. Good, Otto, good. Tell them we'll have our first session after lunch. Show them the lake, the stables, the arts and crafts center, the tennis courts, the boutique. The grand tour, Otto.

OTTO. I could give Mrs. Pitt a rubdown, maybe?

DR. PEPPER. No, Otto.

OTTO. Whirlpool?

DR. PEPPER. Nothing, Otto. Just the tour.

OTTO. I could give Mr. Pitt a rubdown, maybe?

DR. PEPPER. Not yet, Otto. You'll have your turn with both of them.

OTTO. Okay. Ze usual? *(He takes Dr. Pepper's empty glass.)*
DR. PEPPER. Last call, Mrs. Scupp.
DOLLY. I'll have a Tab, maybe.
OTTO. *Nein Tab.*
DOLLY. A Fresca?
OTTO. *Nein Fresca.*
DOLLY. Anything dietetic.
OTTO. *Nichts dietetic, nichts.*
DOLLY. All right, water then.
OTTO. *Wasser?*
DR. PEPPER. *Wasser fur das frau!*
OTTO. *Jawohl, Herr Doktor.*
DR. PEPPER. *(Otto has turned to go.)* Und Otto! Dry-lich! Dry-lich! Dry-lich fur ze martini!
OTTO. *Jawohl, Herr Doktor. (Otto exits.)*
DR. PEPPER. It's an extraordinary race. Is Scupp German?
DOLLY. We don't know what it is.
DR. PEPPER. Good. Then I can say it: I can't stand them. It was a German who incapacitated me.
DOLLY. The Second World War?
DR. PEPPER. My first wife. She pushed me down a short but lethal flight of stairs backstage at the Academy of Music in Philadelphia. So much for the City of Brotherly Love.
DOLLY. How horrible!
DR. PEPPER. It was the single most shattering experience of my life.
DOLLY. But why would anyone do such a thing?
DR. PEPPER. In Roberta's case it was self-defense.
DOLLY. You mean you tried to kill her first?
DR. PEPPER. Only symbolically but my intention was lethal.
DOLLY. So, it would seem, was hers! I've got goosebumps.
DR. PEPPER. It's funny how no one ever asks why it was a flight of stairs backstage at the Academy of Music; you must admit, it's not your usual place for an attempted homicide. My wife was a lieder singer. She'd just given an all-Hugo Wolf recital. She asked me how I thought it went and I said, "Maybe the only thing in the world more boring than an all-Hugo Wolf recital is your singing of an all-Hugo Wolf recital."

The remark just kind of popped out of me and when it popped, she pushed and down I went. Four short steps and here I am. Don't look so tragic, Mrs. Scupp. No Roberta Weismuller and her all-Hugo Wolf recital and no Dunelawn. We divorced, naturally, and she remarried some California grape-grower. Otto used to accompany her. Now Otto accompanies me. Having been unsuccessful in my own marriage, hopefully I can help others to solve their difficulties. Friendly coaching from the marital sidelines.

DOLLY. You never remarried?

DR. PEPPER. You've got to be kidding. The third and fourth toes of your left foot, wasn't it?

DOLLY. The second and third of the right.

DR. PEPPER. Accidents will happen.

DOLLY. Not with a remote-control lawn mower, doctor. It was deliberate.

DR. PEPPER. Those things are devils.

DOLLY. I was dozing by our pool. Harry was on the porch controlling it. I never had a chance.

DR. PEPPER. He didn't go into specific details.

DOLLY. I'm sure he didn't. That's why he's here.

DR. PEPPER. He only said there'd been a slight accident and that was why you hadn't come with him.

DOLLY. A slight accident! Two toes, doctor.

DR. PEPPER. Two legs, Dolly. Do you hear me complaining?

DOLLY. I'm sorry, but I can't afford to take any more chances with a man like that.

DR. PEPPER. That's what marriage is, Mrs. Scupp. One big glorious crap shoot.

DOLLY. Not with a husband who runs you over with a lawn mower, it isn't. That's insanity.

DR. PEPPER. Well you're just in time. Harry's about ready to leave Dunelawn. (Hiram Spane enters. He is in a long bathrobe, beach sandals and wearing sunglasses. He goes to the mini-bar and pours orange juice and champagne into the same glass.) He'll be along shortly. You can see for yourself. If you'll excuse me. Duty calls. Good morning, Hiram.

HIRAM. Morning? I was hoping it was late afternoon. I

haven't been up this early since I saw Mother off on the Graf Zeppelin.

DR. PEPPER. I'm sure you never saw anyone off on the Graf Zeppelin, Hiram.

HIRAM. Well it was something big that moved and it drifted off with her on it. Now I remember, of course! It was the Andrea Doria.

DOLLY. Did she go down with it?

HIRAM. Cornelia Margaret Spane, my mother, never went down with or on anything, including Walter Delano Spane, my father. I don't believe we've been introduced. Bitch.

DR. PEPPER. This is Dolly Scupp, Hiram.

HIRAM. I don't care if it's Dolly Madison. I hate pushy women.

DR. PEPPER. Harry's wife!

HIRAM. Harry? Our Harry? Well why didn't you say so! *(Greeting Dolly warmly.)* How do you do, Mrs. Scupp. I'm sorry, you're not a bitch and I'm only a bitch when I've got a head on me like this one. I have Ethel Merman singing the Immolation Scene in here, the whole thing. I thought *I* mixed a wicked vodka stinger! Who did your husband study bartending with! Lillian Roth?

DOLLY. Harry? Drinking? My Harry? Harry Scupp?

HIRAM. I understand AA has a warrant out for his arrest.

DOLLY. I don't think we're talking about the same Harry Scupp.

HIRAM. The way I feel this morning, we're probably not!

DR. PEPPER. Why don't you take that dip now, Hiram? Mrs. Scupp and I are in the middle of an intake.

HIRAM. Good idea, Jason. With any luck, maybe I'll drown. Do you like to swim, Mrs. Scupp?

DOLLY. I used to before my accident.

HIRAM. Harry said you never knew what hit you. Come on, I don't like to swim alone. I believe in the Buddy System.

DOLLY. I didn't bring a suit.

HIRAM. That never stopped anyone around this place. What do you think I've got on under here?

DOLLY. I blush to think.

HIRAM. You blush to think? I've got to live with it! *(He exits toward the lake.)*

DR. PEPPER. Hiram Spane of the Newport Spanes. They own everything.

DOLLY. Is he a patient here?

DR. PEPPER. Hiram's been a patient here since I founded Dunelawn.

DOLLY. What's his problem?

DR. PEPPER. You're looking at him.

DOLLY. Oh my God! *(Francis Tear enters. He is wearing a bathing cap, a bathrobe and rubber bathing shoes. He pours himself a glass of orange juice.)*

DR. PEPPER. Francis Tear of the Baltimore Tears. They made their fortune in toilet paper.

DOLLY. Someone had to do it.

DR. PEPPER. Good morning, Francis! You just missed each other.

FRANCIS. We're not speaking today.

DR. PEPPER. You and I?

FRANCIS. Hiram and me. He said something very cutting to me last night. Hurt me to the quick, he did. I don't think I'm ready to forgive him yet.

DR. PEPPER. Fine, fine. There's no point in rushing these things.

FRANCIS. *(To Dolly.)* Do you think I look like an embryo, madam?

DOLLY. Why of course not.

FRANCIS. Thank you.

DR. PEPPER. This is Mrs. Scupp, Francis.

FRANCIS. Hello.

DR. PEPPER. Harry Scupp's wife.

FRANCIS. Well I didn't think it was his mother. I'm Francis Tear of the Baltimore Tears. We made our fortune in toilet paper.

DOLLY. Yes, I know.

FRANCIS. Someone had to do it.

DOLLY. So we were just saying.

FRANCIS. What are you in?

20

DOLLY.   I'm just a housewife.

FRANCIS.   So's Hiram! He's also in distress. Psychic distress, doctor!

DR. PEPPER.   Not now, Francis. Take your swim. I like your new bathing slippers.

FRANCIS.   Do you? Hiram's mother had them sent. Hiram's mother has everything sent.

DOLLY.   How nice for you and Hiram.

FRANCIS.   You never met Hiram's mother. You don't think I look sissy in these, Jason?

DR. PEPPER.   Not at all.

FRANCIS.   Do you, Mrs. Scupp?

DOLLY.   They go with the cap.

FRANCIS.   That's what I was hoping. I think it's important to look your best at all times. You never know. Ta ta, then. It must be Jewish, Scupp.

DOLLY.   I was telling Jason, we don't know what it is.

FRANCIS.   It's Jewish. *(He exits.)*

DR. PEPPER.   Eighteen years they've been together, ever since Grey Gables.

DOLLY.   Grey Gables?

DR. PEPPER.   A military academy just north of Ithaca. I believe William F. Buckley is a graduate.

DOLLY.   Are they...?

DR. PEPPER.   I don't think so, but if they are, I'd like to be a fly on that wall. No, I think they're just old, old friends and chamber music partners.

DOLLY.   I didn't know you treated male couples at Dune-lawn.

DR. PEPPER.   We'd treat mules if they could afford it. Love is where you find it.

DOLLY.   That's true.

DR. PEPPER.   Don't be blind, it's all around you, every-where.

PUBLIC ADDRESS SYSTEM.   Premature Ejaculation, Prob-lem or Cop Out? is the topic for this afternoon's discussion under the Great Elm on South Lawn. *(Otto returns with the drinks.)*

21

DOLLY.   Thank you.

DR. PEPPER.   *Danke,* Otto.

OTTO.   Ze *hausfrau* would like a rubdown, maybe?

DOLLY.   I don't think so.

OTTO.   *(Shrugging.)* Okay. *(He takes a magazine off a side table and begins to read.)*

DR. PEPPER.   Cheers! You were saying?

DOLLY.   *(Nodding towards Otto.)* Doctor...!

DR. PEPPER.   Don't mind Otto. It would take a lot more than Harry and your lawnmower to get his nose out of *Opera News.*

DOLLY.   Why did my husband try to kill me?

DR. PEPPER.   Do you still want to talk turkey, Mrs. Scupp?

DOLLY.   About Harry? Of course I do.

DR. PEPPER.   About you.

DOLLY.   What is that supposed to mean?

DR. PEPPER.   Does Labor Day weekend, the parking lot outside Betty's Clam Box in Rockport, Maine, do anything for you?

DOLLY.   I don't know. Should it?

DR. PEPPER.   Think hard.

DOLLY.   Betty's Clam Box?

DR. PEPPER.   Harry was getting something out of the trunk of the car and you put the car into reverse.

DOLLY.   Oh, that! Leave it to Harry to tell you about a silly little accident like that.

DR. PEPPER.   He was in traction for two months.

DOLLY.   I didn't see him back there.

DOLLY.   Eight months later you ran him over with a golf cart at the Westchester Country Club.

DOLLY.   It was an accident. My foot got stuck on the accelerator. I was wearing new golf shoes.

DR. PEPPER.   Nobody drives a golf cart on the putting green.

DOLLY.   I do!

DR. PEPPER.   That time he was in traction for three months.

DOLLY.   You're making mountains out of mole hills, doctor.

DR. PEPPER.   Let's talk about the incident on the archery field.

22

DOLLY. Let's not.

DR. PEPPER. You were using a deer-hunter's crossbow with telescopic sights.

DOLLY. I didn't tell him to change the target when he did.

DR. PEPPER. And what about his high dive in Acapulco?

DOLLY. He *fell.*

DR. PEPPER. Eight hundred and seventy-two feet. And what about your safari to East Africa last winter?

DOLLY. I was delirious. The heat, the water, a touch of malaria. I mistook him for something else.

DR. PEPPER. Just another gorilla in the mist, I suppose.

DOLLY. I don't want to hear these things.

DR. PEPPER. You said you wanted to talk turkey, Mrs. Scupp.

DOLLY. I changed my mind.

DR. PEPPER. Too late. Now here's the turkey: you and your husband have been trying to kill one another since Betty's Clam Box. Why?

DOLLY. Has he been neat, doctor?

DR. PEPPER. Neat?

DOLLY. Neat. Tidy.

DR. PEPPER. Oh, neat! A little over-fastidious perhaps when he got here but—.

DOLLY. I'm talking about the coasters, doctor.

DR. PEPPER. The Coasters?

DOLLY. Those things you put under glasses so they don't leave a ring.

DR. PEPPER. Oh, those coasters. I was thinking of my favorite singing group. *(He sings a phrase of a Coasters hit.)* I'm sorry.

DOLLY. How do you feel about coasters, doctor?

DR. PEPPER. I can't stand them. Always sticking to the bottom of your glass and then dropping off.

DOLLY. I loathe coasters.

DR. PEPPER. I loathe people who follow you around with them.

DOLLY. Then you loathe Harry.

DR. PEPPER. I don't follow.

DOLLY. Harry is the king of coasters. He adores coasters.

He lives coasters. He *is* coasters. Doctor, I can be downstairs in the den watching television late at night and he'll get up upstairs and come down with a coaster for my glass. He wakes up at three a.m. having a nightmare I'm making rings.

DR. PEPPER.   Well are you?

DOLLY.   Of course I am! Wouldn't you? Doctor, this is a man who goes into my closet and straightens my shoes.

DR. PEPPER.   Well that's something. Usually they wear them.

DOLLY.   I wish he would. Maybe he'd break a leg bringing me another one of his goddam coasters! I bet you put your toilet paper on wrong, too.

DR. PEPPER.   I beg your pardon, Mrs. Scupp!

DOLLY.   Did you know you could put a roll of toilet paper on the dispenser wrong? I didn't until I married Harry. "Dolly, how many times do I have to tell you? The paper should roll *under* from the inside *out,* not *over* from the outside *down!*"

DR. PEPPER.   Over from the inside down?

DOLLY.   I try, but I can't remember!

DR. PEPPER.   Under from the outside out?

DOLLY.   He won't let me have down cushions in the house. They crush, he says. Of course they crush; that's why they're comfortable. We're into total foam rubber. I hate foam rubber.

DR. PEPPER.   I'm allergic to it.

DOLLY.   I'm up to my ass in it. Doctor, this is a man who goes around straightening other people's license plates in public parking lots.

DR. PEPPER.   Now surely, Mrs. Scupp!

DOLLY.   If they're dirty, he takes out his handkerchief and cleans them.

DR. PEPPER.   What about in bed?

DOLLY.   Pajamas, tops and bottoms, what do you think?

DR. PEPPER.   I mean, what's he like in bed?

DOLLY.   I don't remember. His hobby is tropical fish. I hate tropical fish.

DR. PEPPER.   You hate tropical fish?

DOLLY. There's something about them. Maybe it's the fact he talks to them. Or the names he gives them. Eric, Tony, Pinky. There's one round, mean-looking one he calls Dolly. I don't take it as a compliment. When they die he buries them. We're the only house in Larchmont with a tropical fish cemetery in the backyard. I'm a mature, sensible and, I think, rather intelligent woman and I hate those fish. You know something else I hate? Stereo equipment. Harry's got woofers, weefers, tweeters, baffles, pre-amps, post-amps, digital this, digital that. He puts gloves on when he handles that equipment. Don't get me started, doctor. There's so many things about Harry I hate. I hate his black Volvo station wagon with the snow tires on in August. He's worried about an early winter. He worries about everything. We're the only people in Larchmont with locust insurance. And try taking a trip with him! He reads road signs. Every road sign. Out loud. "Soft shoulders, Dolly." "Slippery when wet, Dolly." "Deer crossing, Dolly." "Kiwanis Club meetings Wednesday at noon, Dolly." Who gives a good goddamn? He's not even a member of the Kiwanis Club. Who'd want him? Triple A turned him down. Don't get me wrong, doctor, I love my husband. I just can't stand him. That incident with the lawnmower was just the straw that broke the camel's back.

DR. PEPPER. And a very attractive camel she is, too.

DOLLY. Thank you.

OTTO. Rubdown, *Frau Scupp?*

DR. PEPPER. *Nichts!*

OTTO. Okay.

DR. PEPPER. Listen to me, Mrs. Scupp. I can't promise you a happy marriage. I'm not even certain I believe in them. I'm famous for successful marriages for people who want to be married. I think I can help you but you have to want me to help you.

DOLLY. I do. At least, I think I do. *(Harry Scupp is heard calling for Otto off.)*

DR. PEPPER. Harry's coming.

DOLLY. It's just like in a play.

DR. PEPPER. I've done all I can for him. It's up to you now.

DOLLY. I'm frightened.

DR. PEPPER. Given your track record, Mrs. Scupp, I think your husband is the one who should be apprehensive. (*Harry bounds on. He, too, is dressed for swimming, although his ensemble is a good deal less conservative than Hiram or Francis'. He is carrying a small box.*)

HARRY. Otto! Otto! *Wo bist du, Otto?* Good morning, Jason. I'm learning German. Ask me why.

DR. PEPPER. Why?

HARRY. Why not? Life, *ich liebe dich!*

DOLLY. Hello, Harry.

HARRY. Dolly! Doll. Doll Baby! This is terrific. This is great. (*He is advancing on her with open arms.*)

DOLLY. Put me down, Harry! Don't twirl me. My back. Your back. Harry, you're crushing me. I can't breathe.

HARRY. I could eat you alive. Shut up, woman. (*He gives her a very long, very passionate, very deep kiss. Even Dr. Pepper and Otto are a little embarrassed by the intensity of it. Dolly is profoundly shaken.*) They didn't tell me you were coming up.

DOLLY. They didn't know.

HARRY. What a great surprise!

DOLLY. I hope so.

HARRY. Are you kidding? I've been up here so long even Hiram and Francis were starting to look good to me. So was Martin Borman over there. *Gut morgen, Otto.*

OTTO. *Gut morgen, Herr Scupp. Ze usual?*

HARRY. What time is it? It's early. I better stick with the Bloody Marys. Hot, Otto. Very, very hot. *Beaucoup* Tabasco and lots of the white stuff.

OTTO. *Jawohl, Herr Scupp.*

DOLLY. Harry!

HARRY. Otto makes a fantastic Bloody Mary. Takes the top of your head right off and leaves it there.

DOLLY. When did you start drinking?

HARRY. About five minutes after I got here. Kidding, kidding. Lighten up, honey.

DR. PEPPER. Last call, Mrs. Scupp. (*Dolly nods.*) *Bitte, Otto.* (*He holds up his martini glass. Otto nods and exits.*)

HARRY. You look wonderful, Dolly.

DOLLY. Thank you.

HARRY. Doesn't she look wonderful, Jason?

DR. PEPPER. That's just what I've been telling her.

HARRY. Of course, you don't know what she looked like before!

DOLLY. I've lost a little weight.

HARRY. I can see where, too.

DOLLY. You certainly haven't.

HARRY. It's that high-cholesterol diet they've got me on.

DOLLY. You're meant to be on low-cholesterol.

HARRY. Talk to my doctor!

DR. PEPPER. Harry likes high-cholesterol.

HARRY. I never thought I'd actually get tired of Eggs Benedict, chocolate mousse and *creme brulee. (Music is heard off: a Scott Joplin piano rag. It is coming from the main house.)*

DR. PEPPER. Ah, Senor Wences is awake! If you'll excuse me for a few minutes? I want to go over the results of his MPDT with him.

DOLLY. His MPDT?

DR. PEPPER. Multiple Personality Disorder Test.

HARRY. It's a corker, Dolly! You should take one.

DR. PEPPER. I'll let you two get re-acquainted.

DOLLY. *(Anxiously.)* But you're coming back?

DR. PEPPER. Absolutely. There's a security alarm, just in case. *(He laughs.)* Harry's right. Lighten up, Mrs. Scupp. *(Dr. Pepper rolls off-stage. Awkward pause between Dolly and Harry. They listen to the music.)*

HARRY. Boy, that's a real toe-tapper! I'm sorry, honey. How are the kids?

DOLLY. They're fine.

HARRY. Yeah?

DOLLY. Little Eva has an all-county intramural girls wrestling tournament coming up and young Harry was elected president of his Future Homemakers of America chapter.

HARRY. That's great. That's just great.

DOLLY. They need a father, Harry.

HARRY. Do they miss me?

27

DOLLY. Of course they miss you. I miss you.

HARRY. That's great. That's just great.

DOLLY. I've got your magazines in the car.

HARRY. My *Hi-Fi Stereo Reviews*?

DOLLY. And your *Popular Aquariums*.

HARRY. Thank you.

DOLLY. And the summer pajamas you wrote for.

HARRY. My blue cottons with the penguins?

DOLLY. I thought you meant your yellow drip-drys with the sailboats!

HARRY. No, I meant my blue cottons with the penguins.

DOLLY. I'm sorry.

HARRY. That's okay.

DOLLY. I could drive back and —!

HARRY. Really, it doesn't matter. *(The piano rag stops.)*

DOLLY. It's a pleasant drive up here.

HARRY. I hope you read those warning signs on that bypass outside of Inglenook.

DOLLY. Oh, I did! I thought of you when I saw them.

HARRY. An average of thirteen and a half people get killed there every year.

DOLLY. I'll be extra careful on the way back.

HARRY. When are you leaving?

DOLLY. I don't know. It depends.

HARRY. I hope you'll stay for the Talent Show. Larry Mullens and I are doing the Tent Scene from *Julius Caesar.* "Hah! Portia dead? How 'scaped I killing when I crossed thee thus?!"

DOLLY. We'll see. What's in the box?

HARRY. Henry.

DOLLY. Henry?

HARRY. My angel fish.

DOLLY. What happened?

HARRY. Evelyn killed him.

DOLLY. Who's Evelyn?

HARRY. My electric eel.

DOLLY. That's awful.

HARRY. It's only a fish. *(He tosses the box away.)*

DOLLY. You always used to give them such nice burials.

HARRY. I must be getting cynical in my old age. *(Short pause.)* I guess you sold the lawnmower.

DOLLY. No. It's in the garage waiting for you.

HARRY. That's great. That's really great.

DOLLY. It's broken, of course.

HARRY. I wasn't really trying to get you with it.

DOLLY. Yes, you were, Harry. Why?

HARRY. There were a million reasons. It was hot. The Gypsy Moths were eating the elms. The charcoal grill needed cleaning. The car keys were upstairs when they should have been downstairs. There was a new water ring on the telephone stand. You know, honey. Things like that.

DOLLY. Did I have the toilet paper on right at least?

HARRY. As a matter of fact, you did. What happened?

DOLLY. I don't know. I lost my head!

HARRY. Only someone had been playing with the stereo. There were fingerprints on my Burl Ives Christmas album.

DOLLY. Why were you listening to a Christmas album in August?

HARRY. I wasn't. I just happened to be doing my six-month record cleaning that day. It's all right, honey. They weren't your fingerprints.

DOLLY. Thank you.

HARRY. They weren't the kids' either.

DOLLY. I'm just glad I had the toilet paper on right.

HARRY. I conceded that point.

DOLLY. Well?

HARRY. It was blue.

DOLLY. That's all they had.

HARRY. It was blue! Our bathroom is red! Everything is red. The sink, the tub, the tile, the towels, the shower curtain! You know I don't like a clash. I like everything to match.

DOLLY. Blue was all they had.

HARRY. You asked me why, cupcake. I'm telling you why. There were permanent press sheets on the bed.

DOLLY. Ralph Lauren!

HARRY. I don't care if they were Sophia Loren. I can't sleep on permanent press. They're too hot. They're like flame sheets. And then, when I saw you staked out by the pool in your bathing suit drinking an iced tea without a coaster, I just kind of lost control with the mower. Like I said, it was hot. There were a million reasons. What was it with me?

DOLLY.   The coasters.

HARRY.   I thought Betty's Clam Box was something I'd said.

DOLLY.   It was the coasters.

HARRY.   Even that time in Acapulco?

DOLLY.   It was always the coasters.

HARRY.   I wasn't going to mention it, Dolly, but.... *(He motions towards Dolly's glass.)*

DOLLY.   I'm sorry. *(She looks for a coaster to set it on.)*

HARRY.   It's okay, it's okay! *(He takes the glass from her and puts it on the table without a coaster.)* Make all the rings you want, Dolly. No problem. *No hay problema!*

DOLLY.   Dr. Pepper seems to think you're ready to go home.

HARRY.   *(Taking out a cigarette.)* He's done wonders for me, Doll.

DOLLY.   When did you take that up?

HARRY.   A couple of months ago. You want one?

DOLLY.   No, thank you.

HARRY.   They're fertilized with chicken shit, honey.

DOLLY.   I know! *(Otto has returned with their drinks.)*

HARRY.   Thanks, Otto.

OTTO.   Rubdown, *Herr Scupp?*

HARRY.   Not just now, Otto, maybe later. Dolly?

DOLLY.   I don't think so.

HARRY.   Thanks anyway, Otto.

OTTO.   Okay. *(He exits.)*

HARRY.   That man has magic fingers. He's taken my id and put it where my angst used to be.

DOLLY.   Maybe that explains it. You look terrible, Harry.

HARRY.   I'm a little hung over this morning.

DOLLY.   What from?

HARRY.   Margaritas. They're vicious, Dolly. Stay away from 'em.

DOLLY.   What were you doing drinking margaritas?

HARRY. The Plungs.

DOLLY. Who or what are the Plungs?

HARRY. Jeanine and Billy Plung. This young couple from Roanoke Jason was treating for S&M I got friendly with while they were up here. We had a little farewell party for them last night. Jeanine had me dancing the Merengue with her until nearly three.

DOLLY. You can't Merengue, Harry. You can't even boxstep.

HARRY. I can now.

DOLLY. I thought they were taking care of you up here.

HARRY. They are. I never felt better in my life.

DOLLY. S&M?

HARRY. It stands for sado-masochism.

DOLLY. I know what S&M is.

HARRY. I sure didn't. My jaw must have been down to here. I didn't know people did things like that to one another.

DOLLY. How old was this woman?

HARRY. Twenty-two, twenty-three.

DOLLY. Harry, what's gotten into you?

HARRY. I'm my old self again. It's me, Harry Scupp with the bright red T-Bird and a six-pack and let the good times roll and "Beat Port Chester, Larchmont!" and Studio Fifty-Two and Dolly Veasey is my number one date. It's gonna be like old times again, Doll.

DOLLY. We never had old times like that.

HARRY. It's never too late.

DOLLY. You never had a red Thunderbird. We took the bus. And it's Studio Fifty-Four, Harry. They never once let us in.

HARRY. I'm talking about life, Dolly. *Joie de vivre!*

DOLLY. And what do you mean, "your old self?"

HARRY. I love you. I don't want to kill you anymore. Do you want to see what I've been doing since I've been here?

DOLLY. Yes! No! I don't know! What!

HARRY. Close your eyes.

DOLLY. Why?

HARRY. I'm not going to hit you. I want to show you something. It's a surprise. Are they closed?

DOLLY. Yes.

31

HARRY. I'll be right back. *(He rushes off.)*

PUBLIC ADDRESS SYSTEM. MEN WHO CAN'T COME AND THE WOMEN WHO CAN WHO LOVE THEM will be the topic of Dr. Pepper's talk this afternoon at 4 in Liszt Hall. Refreshments and moist towelettes will be available.

DOLLY. Hurry up, Harry, I don't like this. *(She opens her eyes just as Otto re-appears crossing on his way to the lake for a swim. Otto is in a bikini. Dolly screams at the sight of him, then closes her eyes again.)*

HARRY. *(Off.)* It's incredible that you should be here today. I just finished this last night. *(Harry rushes back on. He is excited and out of breath. He carries an object.)* Okay, Doll, open. *(Dolly opens her eyes. Harry hands her the object.)*

DOLLY. What is it?

HARRY. An ashtray.

DOLLY. An ashtray?

HARRY. Isn't it pretty? I mean, did you know I had a sensitivity like that all bottled up inside me? I didn't.

DOLLY. Are you sure it's an ashtray?

HARRY. It's a nude study of Jeanine.

DOLLY. Jeanine Plung?

HARRY. I love that line there, don't you?

DOLLY. Harry, this woman is naked!

HARRY. How else do you sculpt a nude, honey? She did one of me she's thinking of turning into a lamp.

DOLLY. What you're suggesting, Harry, is that you were somewhat more than just friends with these people.

HARRY. Oh, I was! You'll go crazy over them and vice-versa.

DOLLY. I wouldn't count on it. And what do you mean, I'll *go* crazy over them?

HARRY. I invited them for Thanksgiving. Now wait right here. There's something else I want to show you.

DOLLY. Billy Plung as a hat rack!

HARRY. Don't move. *(He runs off.)*

DOLLY. Doctor! *(Dr. Pepper emerges at once from behind the hedges. Clearly, he has been listening to their conversation.)* What have you done to him?

DR. PEPPER. What do you think of the change?

DOLLY.   I hate it!

DR. PEPPER.   He's called you "honey" several times at least.

DOLLY.   "They're loaded with chicken shit, honey" were his exact words.

DR. PEPPER.   *(Proferring his pack.)* You're sure you still won't have one?

DOLLY.   Now what about Harry and these Plung people?

DR. PEPPER.   Just Mrs. Plung.

DOLLY.   And where was Mr. Plung for all this?

DR. PEPPER.   Rumor has it with Otto.

DOLLY.   I wouldn't be surprised.

DR. PEPPER.   Really? I was flabbergasted.

DOLLY.   And you just allowed all this to happen?

DR. PEPPER.   There are no rules at Dunelawn, Mrs. Scupp. I steer people in search of strict discipline across the lake to Ravenswood and my arch rival and nemesis, Dr. Lionel Toynbee. *(He shudders.)*

DOLLY.   What's wrong?

DR. PEPPER.   I shudder every time I hear those names. Ravenswood. *(He shudders.)* Dr. Toynbee. *(He shudders again.)* Where were we?

DOLLY.   You can stand there — I mean, sit there and tell me you let my husband go off into the woods —.

DR. PEPPER.   *Into The Woods?* Did you like that show? "No One Is Alone." What does that *mean*, exactly? I'm sorry.

DOLLY.   — with that horrible Plung woman!

DR. PEPPER.   How did you know she was horrible? I thought I'd kept that to myself. She's a dreadful woman. I don't know what Harry saw in her. He would've been better off with Otto.

DOLLY.   I'm beginning to think you made my husband do all these horrible things.

DR. PEPPER.   I've never made anyone do anything, Mrs. Scupp. The secret of my success here at Dunelawn, such as it is, is that I allow everyone to do exactly as they please.

DOLLY.   At your prices, I'd hardly call that a bargain.

DR. PEPPER.   You'd be surprised how few people know what it is they truly want.

DOLLY.   I know what I want.

DR. PEPPER.   Do you, Mrs. Scupp?

DOLLY.   At least I thought I did until I saw Harry like this! *(Harry rushes back on, Otto following at a slight distance. Harry carries a ukulele and a tap board. He has put on tap shoes and is wearing a black silk top hat and is carrying an ivory-tip cane. Otto brings on a set of drums, complete with foot-pedal and a battery of cymbals.)*

HARRY.   I'll bet you didn't know I was a frustrated song-and-dance man, did you, Doll? You're really going to get a kick out of this. Sit down. You know how I always overdo things at first? That's because of my masculine insecurity coming out. I didn't even know I was masculinely insecure until Jason here got his hands on me. *(He tousles Dr. Pepper's hair.)* Well, honey... *(Dr. Pepper catches Dolly's eye.)*

DR. PEPPER.   *(Holding up fingers.)* That's the seventh time!

HARRY.   ...it turns out I've got a singing voice. And dancing feet, too! I've got rhythm, Dolly. I said, sit down. I want you to see this. *(Harry hands Dr. Pepper the ukelele. Otto is already stationed at the drums. Harry looks to each and gives the downbeat.)* Five, six, seven, eight! *(They launch into a lively song. It's obvious they've been practicing. They're not at all half bad, actually. Dolly watches with growing discomfort.)*

DOLLY.   Stop it! I can't stand seeing you like this!

HARRY.   I told you it was a new me. Five, six, seven, eight!

DOLLY.   Singing, dancing, smoking, drinking! Making ashtrays!

HARRY.   You ain't seen nothing yet! Wait'll they see this at the Westchester Country Club. I said, five, six, seven, eight! *(He launches back into the song, Dr. Pepper and Otto accompanying him. This time, their big finish is even bigger than before. Harry ends down on one knee, his arms open wide, ready for approval. Dolly hurls the ashtray at him, barely missing him.)*

DOLLY.   I'm taking you home.

HARRY.   You broke my ashtray.

DOLLY.   You came here to get better.

HARRY.   You broke my ashtray.

DOLLY.   You're getting worse.

HARRY.   You broke my ashtray!! *(Harry is advancing on her.*

Dolly is getting something out of her purse.)
DR. PEPPER.   Get her, Harry!
HARRY.   YOU BROKE MY ASHTRAY!
DOLLY.   *(Holding up a small cylinder.)* One more step, Harry, and I'll squirt!   *(Hiram and Francis are heard off-stage calling to Harry from the lakeside.)*
HIRAM and FRANCIS.   *(Off.)* Harry! Harry! Harry Scupp! Last one in's a rotten egg!
HARRY.   I promised Hiram and Francis I'd race them out to the raft. They're like kids that way. They'll keep it up all morning until I do. *(To Dr. Pepper.)* See if you can help her, Jason. *(He bursts into tears.)*
DR. PEPPER.   I'll do my best. *(Harry runs off to the lake. Dolly is trembling.)* Excuse me, but what is that?
DOLLY.   Oh, it's just Mace. It blinds and stuns your attacker. You just push here and—! I'm sorry!
DR. PEPPER.   It's too bad my wife didn't carry one of those. Too bad for me, that is.
DOLLY.   You said he was better, doctor!
DR. PEPPER.   You still don't see the change!
DOLLY.   Not the change I want!
DR. PEPPER.   Harry loved that piece of sculpture.
DOLLY.   I hate it!
DR. PEPPER.   I hope you're listening to yourself.
DOLLY.   What have you done to him?
DR. PEPPER.   No, Harry's done it to himself. Maybe it's your turn now.
DOLLY.   And maybe it isn't! Everything was fine until you got into the act. Terrible but fine.
DR. PEPPER.   Know what you want, Mrs. Scupp. That's the first step.
DOLLY.   I want what anyone wants. I want a good marriage.
DR. PEPPER.   Fair enough. Give me three months.
DOLLY.   And I want to be happy.
DR. PEPPER.   Better make it three and a half.
DOLLY.   And I want sexual fulfillment.
DR. PEPPER.   From your lips to the Big Fellow's big ears!
DOLLY.   That's not much, is it?

35

DR. PEPPER. It's everything. Now: it's a beautiful summer's day, God's in his Heaven and all's right with the world. Harry will be waiting for you down by the lake. I'd go to him if I were you.

DOLLY. I'm still a little frightened to be alone with him.

DR. PEPPER. Just whistle and Otto will be down there in a flash.

OTTO. *Jawohl, frau.* Like a stag!

DR. PEPPER. You know how to whistle, don't you?

DOLLY. You put your lips together and blow.

DR. PEPPER. I think we can work together.

DOLLY. With my foot like this, I can't go swimming. Maybe I could ask him to take me out in a canoe.

DR. PEPPER. I wouldn't push my luck. Try skipping stones, Mrs. Scupp.

DOLLY. It's Dolly. Please. Call me Dolly.

DR. PEPPER. Okay, Dolly.

DOLLY. I knew this would happen! It always does!

DR. PEPPER. I think I know what you're going to say.

DOLLY. I always get a crush on doctors! *(Dolly exits.)*

DR. PEPPER. That's not at all what I thought she was going to say.

OTTO. Crush? *Was ist* crush?

DR. PEPPER. Mrs. Scupp thinks she likes me.

OTTO. Everyone likes *Herr Doktor. (He laughs his jovial laugh.)*

DR. PEPPER. That's because everyone thinks *Herr Doktor* likes them. *(He sits smoking and sipping his martini. Otto is clearing up the tap board and drum set and re-arranging the drinks cart. As he works, he sings.)*

DR. PEPPER. You're singing my favorite song again, Otto.

OTTO. *Ja.* My mother used to sing this song.

DR. PEPPER. It's a beauty.

OTTO. My mother was a pig. She smoked cigars and wouldn't change my diaper. Her favorite singer was Bing Crosby. It was terrible. I had to do what I did. I had to, I had to!

DR. PEPPER. I know. I know. *(A tennis ball bounces onto the terrace and lands at Dr. Pepper's feet.)*

ROY. *(Off.)* Hey, Mac, you want to send that back?

APRIL. *(Off.)* We're talking to you, asshole! Send the ball back, you creep!

DR. PEPPER. Otto. *(He points to the ball. Otto returns the ball.)*

ROY. Thank you!

APRIL. Yeah, thanks loads! *(They go back to the tennis court.)*

DR. PEPPER. *Das ists ze newly-weds-Pitt?*

OTTO. *Das ists ze newly-weds-Pitt.*

DR. PEPPER. Oy! *(Holding out his empty glass.) Bitte,* Otto. *(Francis is heard off-stage crowing "We beat you! We beat you!")* Better make that three. *Eins, zwei, drei* cocktails, Otto.

OTTO. *Jawohl. (He exits as Hiram and Francis return from their swim in the lake.)*

DR. PEPPER. Who won?

FRANCIS. *(Singing, skipping almost.)* Harry and me! Harry and me! Harry and me!

HIRAM. They ganged up on me as usual.

FRANCIS. We beat you! We beat you! Da da da we beat you!

HIRAM. Well, Harry beat you.

FRANCIS. And we both beat you!

HIRAM. I was worried about that turtle.

FRANCIS. Even with these on, I beat him. *(Indeed, water is sloshing out of his rubber bathing slippers.)* I beat you! I beat you!

HIRAM. I am going to beat you black and blue if you keep that up, Francis!

DR. PEPPER. Boys, boys!

FRANCIS. I'm still not speaking to you!

HIRAM. That's a blessing!

FRANCIS. But... *(Very softly.)* I beat you! I beat you!

DR. PEPPER. Hiram, did you tell Francis he looked like an embryo?

HIRAM. If I'd seen him in that bathing cap, I'd've said he looked like a prophylactic.

FRANCIS. Hiram is a poor sport! Hiram is a poor sport!

HIRAM. If there's anything more vulgar than swimming, it's a swimming race.

FRANCIS. It was his idea.

37

HIRAM.   Does that sound like me, Jason?

FRANCIS.   It was, too!

HIRAM.   You see what I have to put up with?

FRANCIS.   Last night after dinner you said, "Let's challenge Harry Scupp to a swimming race tomorrow."

HIRAM.   Are you sure you can't do anything for him, Doctor?

FRANCIS.   You did, you did!

HIRAM.   I'd suggest a lobotomy but obviously he's already had one.

FRANCIS.   I cross my heart, he did!

HIRAM.   Several, from the look of it!

FRANCIS.   *(Getting quite hysterical.)* He lies, Doctor, he lies! He did suggest a swimming race after dinner with Harry Scupp last night! He did! He did!

DR. PEPPER.   Don't hold it back, Francis.

FRANCIS.   *(A real tantrum now: feet and fists pounding the ground.)* Tell him! Tell him it was your idea, Hiram! Tell him, tell him, tell him, tell him, tell him, tell him, tell him, tell him! *(He is exhausting himself as Hiram interrupts.)*

HIRAM.   All right! So it *was* my idea. I don't like to lose. It's the Spane in me. A Baltimore Tear wouldn't understand that. *(Genuinely.)* Oh I'm sorry, Francis. *(Francis sulks.)* Now get up. You know I can't stand to see you grovel like that.

FRANCIS.   I'm not grovelling, Hiram. I'm the one letting it all out for a change. Right, Doctor?

DR. PEPPER.   Just keep going. I think we might be getting somewhere.

FRANCIS.   He always wants to compete with me. I can't help it if I always win. I don't even want to win. I just do. Backgammon, bridge, whist, Chinese checkers, Mah-jongg...

HIRAM.   You never beat me at Mah-jongg.

FRANCIS.   Yes, I did. That time in Morocco.

HIRAM.   I don't count that.

FRANCIS.   Why not?

HIRAM.   I had dysentery.

FRANCIS.   So did I!

HIRAM.   I said I was sorry!

FRANCIS.   I always win! At anything! Anagrams, Parcheesi,

Scrabble, tennis...

HIRAM. That's table tennis, Francis!

FRANCIS. Well I win, don't I? Like I always do? I can't lose to him at anything! And he hates me for it! Oh he just hates me to death!

HIRAM. While you're down there crowing, Francis, why don't you tell the doctor the *real* story?

FRANCIS. What real story?

HIRAM. What real story!

FRANCIS. I don't know what you're talking about!

HIRAM. Why don't you tell him about Celine? *(A short pause.)* I didn't think so.

DR. PEPPER. Who is Celine?

HIRAM. A Welsh Corgi we had when we lived on 73rd Street.

DR. PEPPER. It's a lovely little dog.

HIRAM. Francis killed her.

FRANCIS. It was an accident.

HIRAM. He threw her out of the window.

FRANCIS. I didn't throw her out the window. She jumped.

HIRAM. Of course she did!

FRANCIS. You weren't there. She jumped out!

HIRAM. Celine hadn't jumped *anywhere* since Mummy's car backed over her in New Hope three years before! You threw that dog!

FRANCIS. She'd been trying to catch this big fly in her mouth when suddenly she just sailed out the window right after it.

HIRAM. Do you really expect Dr. Pepper to believe that cock and bull story?

FRANCIS. It's true. It's true!

DR. PEPPER. What floor were you on?

FRANCIS. The fourteenth.

HIRAM. The fatal fourteenth.

FRANCIS. I didn't throw her.

HIRAM. Well who left that window open?

FRANCIS. You couldn't breathe that night.

HIRAM. And you were thinking of yourself first, as usual!

DR. PEPPER. No air-conditioning?

FRANCIS.   This was years ago.

HIRAM.   When dog-killers could still get away with something as simple as an open window. God knows what he'd come up with today.

DR. PEPPER.   What a ghastly story.

HIRAM.   Most crimes of passion are. Francis was jealous of her. Celine adored me, couldn't stand him. She used to pee in his closet out of spite. So he killed her.

FRANCIS.   If you say that again I'm going to smack your face for you.

HIRAM.   Say what? You dog murderer! *(Francis flies at him.)*

FRANCIS.   I am not a dog murderer! You take that back!

DR. PEPPER.   Don't hold it back. *(They struggle. They do minor violence to each other.)*

FRANCIS.   Take it back! Take it back, take it back, take it back, take it back, take it back... *(Dr. Pepper, watching from the sidelines, offers encouragement during the encounter.)*

DR. PEPPER.   That's right, boys, let it out. Let it out. No holding back, now. That's right, that's right. Just let everything out now. *(During the struggle Otto returns with the drinks. He looks to Dr. Pepper, who motions him to let the combatants be. Otto shrugs, sits down with his magazine. Finally, Hiram overwhelms Francis and, pinning him down, lightly slaps his face and arm.)*

HIRAM.   Have you lost your mind? Don't you ever lift a hand to me again as long as you live, do you hear me? Ever! Ever, ever, ever, ever, ever. *(One last little slap.)* Ever. *(Hiram and Francis collapse with exhaustion.)*

DR. PEPPER.   All right now?

FRANCIS.   I don't think Dunelawn is working out for us.

HIRAM.   Of course Dunelawn isn't working out for us! Why should it?

DR. PEPPER.   Did you ever think of getting another dog?

HIRAM.   No more dogs. Celine was a terrible shedder.

FRANCIS.   Another one would probably just pee in my closet, too.

HIRAM.   Or maybe mine next time.

FRANCIS.   No more dogs, Hiram? Promise?

HIRAM.   The only reason we stay together is because no one

else in the world would put up with us.

DR. PEPPER.   If you can leave here having realized that much, I'll be satisfied.

HIRAM.   *You'll* be satisfied?

DR. PEPPER.   And so should you.

HIRAM.   We are, I suppose. We are.

FRANCIS.   You're the only real friend I've ever had, Hiram.

HIRAM.   And I'm sure Dr. Pepper can see why. Help me up, will you? I think I twisted something. *(Francis struggles to his feet, then helps Hiram up.)*

FRANCIS.   Are we dressing for lunch?

HIRAM.   I don't know about the end of the Baltimore Tear line but the last remaining Newport Spane is. Otto, where's my Bullshot? *(As they move toward the drinks, another tennis ball bounds across the stage. Roy and April are heard yelling from off-stage.)*

ROY.   *(Off.)* Ball!

APRIL.   *(Off.)* Ball!

ROY.   *Ball!*

APRIL.   *Ball!*

HIRAM.   Who are those dreadful people?

DR. PEPPER.   The Pitts.

FRANCIS.   Pitts? What kind of name is Pitts?

HIRAM.   Appropriate! *(He gulps his Bullshot.)*

APRIL.   Hey, you, Mac, you wanna throw that ball back for Christ's sake?

HIRAM.   My name is not Mac, I'm not your ball boy, and why don't you try fucking yourself, madam! Come on, Francis. *(They exit. Dr. Pepper is alone with the tennis ball.)*

ROY.   *(Running in.)* Hey, you can't talk to my wife life that! *(To April, who is following him.)* Will you please go back there? We'll lose our place on the court.

APRIL.   I'll get the court back! I want to see you handle something for once!

ROY.   I told you: I'm gonna flatten that S.O.B.! Keep the court! Where'd he go?

DR. PEPPER.   Good morning.

ROY.   We saw you talking to him!! Now where is he?

DR. PEPPER. Who?

ROY. The guy who insulted my wife!

DR. PEPPER. Your wife?

APRIL. What do I look like? His trick?

DR. PEPPER. You must be Mr. and Mrs. Pitt.

ROY. Yeah, as a matter of fact, we *are*.

APRIL. And they got some nice class of people up at this place!

ROY. *(Cautioning her.)* Honey! I think we've been recognized.

DR. PEPPER. I'm afraid so.

ROY. Celebrity-time!

APRIL. Oh, Christ!

ROY. *(Taking off his sunglasses and shaking Dr. Pepper's hand.)* Hi, Roy Pitt. Nice to see you. We were hoping to be a little incognito up here! It's just as well. I think actors who wear big sunglasses are big phonies. This is my wife, April James.

APRIL. Hi, April James. Nice to see you.

DR. PEPPER. April James?

APRIL. It's my professional name.

ROY. You see that, honey? Even with these things on he recognized us.

DR. PEPPER. And what do *you* do, Mrs. Pitt?

APRIL. What do you mean, "What do I do?" I'm an actress. Thanks a lot, buddy.

ROY. She's an actress.

APRIL. I don't even know you but I really needed that little ego boost.

ROY. Honey, of course he recognized me. My movie was on the "Late Show" last night. *Cold Fingers*. He probably caught it.

APRIL. God knows you did.

ROY. It's the power of the medium! You know that kind of exposure.

APRIL. *Cold Fingers* should have *opened* on the "Late Show."

ROY. Now don't start with me.

APRIL. Boy, I really needed that little zap.

ROY. He's a dummy.

APRIL. You must have seen me in something. How about *Journey Through Hell* for Christ's sake! You didn't see me in *Journey Through Hell*?

DR. PEPPER. Were you in that?

ROY. That was my beautiful April all right!

APRIL. You bet your sweet ass it was!

DR. PEPPER. That was a wonderful movie, Mrs. Pitt.

APRIL. You see that? Another zap?

ROY. April wasn't in the movie. She created the role off-Broadway ... didn't get the film version!

APRIL. Boy, this is really my day!

ROY. She was brilliant in that part.

APRIL. I know. Too bad the play didn't support me. Try *Random Thoughts and Vaguer Notions*, why don't you?

ROY. That one was on Broadway. April was one of the stars.

DR. PEPPER. I wasn't able to catch it.

APRIL. It ran nearly 20 performances. You didn't exactly have to be a jackrabbit.

ROY. April!

APRIL. Before you zap me again, I didn't do the movie of that one, either.

ROY. You never read notices like she got for that one. Show 'em to him, honey.

APRIL. They're in the car. I break my balls trying to make that piece of shit work and they sign some WASP starlet for the movie version thinking she's going to appeal to that goddamn Middle American drive-in audience.

ROY. I don't really think you can call Bette Midler a WASP starlet.

APRIL. White bread! That's all she is, white bread!

ROY. *(Calling off.)* Hey, that court's taken, Buddy. We got it reserved.

APRIL. You heard him!

DR. PEPPER. I think that's the ground keeper.

ROY. That's okay, Mac! Sorry! Hang in there!

APRIL. Hi! April James! Nice to see you!

ROY. Hi! Roy Pitt! Nice to see you! Ssh! Sssh!

APRIL. What is it?

ROY. I thought I heard our phone.

APRIL. Way out here? What are you? The big ear?

ROY. You sure you told the service where I'd be?

APRIL. Of course I did. I might be getting a call, too, you know.

ROY. I'm expecting a call from the coast. I'm not usually this tense.

APRIL. Hah!

ROY. This could be the big one, April.

APRIL. Almost anything would be bigger than *Cold Fingers.* *(Otto has appeared.)*

ROY. *(Starting to do push-ups.)* You got one hell of a thirsty star out here, waiter.

APRIL. Two thirsty stars.

OTTO. I am not a waiter. My name is Otto.

ROY. Hi, Otto. Roy Pitt, nice to see you.

APRIL. Hi, Otto. April James, nice to see you.

ROY. *(Now he is doing sit-ups.)* What are you having, honey?

APRIL. A screwdriver.

ROY. I'll have some Dom Perignon. The champagne.

APRIL. Roy!

ROY. It's included.

APRIL. Eighty-six the screwdriver. I'll have the same.

OTTO. The *Fraulein* would like a nice rubdown, maybe?

APRIL. From you?

ROY. Just bring the Dom Perignon, will you?

DR. PEPPER. Oh, and Otto! *(He holds up his glass.)*

OTTO. *Jawohl. (He goes.)*

APRIL. *(Sits, and looks at Dr. Pepper's wheelchair for the first time.)* I want to apologize for earlier when we yelled at you for the ball. We didn't realize you were ... like that.

DR. PEPPER. Half the time I don't realize it myself.

APRIL. We do a lot of benefits, you know.

ROY. April's been asked to do the Mental Health and Highway Safety Telethons two years straight.

APRIL. Easter Seals wanted me last month but they weren't paying expenses.

ROY. Nobody's blaming you, honey.

APRIL.   I mean there's charity and then there's charity. I mean you gotta draw the line somewhere, right? What am I? Chopped liver?

ROY.   Easter Seals wouldn't even send a limousine for her! Our agent told them they could take their telethon and shove it. *(Roy is opening up a sun reflector.)*

APRIL.   What are you doing?

ROY.   You don't mind if we don't play tennis for a while? I want to get some of the benefits.

APRIL.   There's not enough sun for a tan.

ROY.   That's what you think. It's a day like this you can really bake yourself. Just because the sky's grey doesn't mean those rays aren't coming through. Make love to me, soleil, make love to me.

APRIL.   *(She is sitting near Dr. Pepper. Roy is sprawled out with his reflector under his chin. He just loves lying in the sun like this.)* What are you in for?

DR. PEPPER.   The usual.

APRIL.   A bad marriage, huh? That's too bad. You're probably wondering what we're doing here. I know on the surface it must look like we got a model marriage. But believe me, we got our little problems, too. Don't look so surprised. Roy's got an ego on him you could drive a mack truck with. Show business marriages ain't nothing to write home about. Half our friends are divorced and the other half are miserable. Naturally, they don't think we're going to make it. Think. They *hope*. But we're going to show them. Right, honey?

ROY.   Right.

APRIL.   Have you had a session with Dr. Pepper yet?

DR. PEPPER.   Many. *(He picks up the book he took from Dolly and opens it.)*

APRIL.   Is he all he's cracked up to be?

DR. PEPPER.   I think so, but of course I'm prejudiced. *(He smiles at April and begins to read.)*

APRIL.   He's gonna have his hands full with that one.

DR. PEPPER.   *(Looking up.)* I'm sorry...?

APRIL.   Skip it. *(Dr. Pepper returns to his book. April silently mouths an obscenity at him and turns her attention to Roy.)*

ROY. Honey! You're blocking my sun.

APRIL. You're just gonna lie there like that?

ROY. Unh-hunh.

APRIL. So where's my reflector?

ROY. I told you to pack it if you wanted it.

APRIL. I want it.

ROY. You said you didn't want to get any darker.

APRIL. I'm starting to fade.

ROY. No, you're not.

APRIL. It's practically all gone. Look at you. You're twice as dark!

ROY. It's not a contest, honey.

APRIL. I mean what's the point of getting a tan if you don't maintain it? Roy!

ROY. *(For Dr. Pepper's benefit, but without looking up from the reflector.)* Do you believe this? I was with my agents all day and I'm supposed to be worried about a goddamn reflector!

APRIL. Just give me a couple of minutes with it.

ROY. It's the best sun time now.

APRIL. You know I've got that audition Wednesday.

ROY. No. N.O. *(April gives up, gets the tin of cocoa butter off the cart and begins applying it.)* April's up for another new musical. They were interested in us both, actually, but I've got these film commitments.

APRIL. Tentative film commitments.

ROY. You're getting hostile, honey.

APRIL. What's hostile is you not packing my reflector.

ROY. *I* was busy with my agents. *You* are getting hostile.

APRIL. I've got a career, too, you know.

ROY. *(Sitting up, he drops the reflector and motions for quiet.)* Ssshh!

APRIL. *(Grabbing the reflector.)* Hello? Yes, we're checking on the availability of Roy Pitt for an Alpo commercial!

ROY. Shut up, April! *(He listens, disappointed.)* Shit. *(Then he sees April.)* Hold it. Stop it! *(He grabs the reflector and lies back.)*

APRIL. Roy!

ROY. After that? You gotta be kidding! I wouldn't give you this reflector if you whistled "Swanee River" out of your ass.

APRIL.   I can, too.

ROY.   I know. I've heard you.

APRIL.   Just lie there and turn into leather.

ROY.   I will.

APRIL.   There are other things in the world more important than your sun tan, you know.

ROY.   Like yours?

APRIL.   For openers.

ROY.   Like your career?

APRIL.   Yes, as a matter of fact.

ROY.   Will you stop competing with me, April? That's one of the reasons we came here. I can't help it if I'm hotter than you right now.

APRIL.   That could change, Roy. Remember James Mason in *A Star is Born?*

ROY.   Well, until it does, love me for what I am: Roy Pitt, the man. But don't resent me for my career.

APRIL.   I know, Roy.

ROY.   I love you for what you are: April James, the best little actress in New York City.

APRIL.   What do you mean, "best little actress"?

ROY.   I'm trying to make a point, honey!

APRIL.   As opposed to what? A dwarf?

ROY.   If we're going to have a good marriage and, April, I want that more than anything...!   *Clayton*

APRIL.   More than you wanted *THE ELEPHANT MAN?*

ROY.   I didn't want *THE ELEPHANT MAN.*

APRIL.   He would've crawled through broken glass for that part!

ROY.   I didn't want *THE ELEPHANT MAN.* Now goddamit, shut up!

APRIL.   I can't talk to you when you get like that.

ROY.   Get like what? You haven't laid off me since we got in the car.

APRIL.   You know I'm upset.

ROY.   We've all been fired from shows.

APRIL.   The same day they went into rehearsal? I'm thinking of slitting the *two* wrists this time, Roy!

47

ROY. Actually, Patti LuPone isn't a bad choice for that part.

APRIL. She's the pits!

ROY. We're the Pitts! *(Breaking himself up, then...)* We liked her in *The Seagull.*

APRIL. You liked her in *The Seagull.* I'd like her in her coffin.

ROY. Obviously they're going ethnic with it.

APRIL. She isn't even ethnic. She's white bread. I'm ethnic. I want a hit, Roy. I need a hit. I'm going crazy for a hit. I mean, when's it my turn?

ROY. Honey, you're making a shadow.

APRIL. I'm sorry.

ROY. That's okay. Just stick with me, kid. We're headed straight for the top.

APRIL. Roy?

ROY. What, angel?

APRIL. Your toupe is slipping. *(Roy clutches at his hairpiece.)* Roy wears a piece.

ROY. It's no secret. I've never pretended. It's not like your nose job!

APRIL. Don't speak to me. Just lie there and turn into naugahyde like your mother!

ROY. Honey! I almost forgot. Your agent called! They're interviewing hostesses for Steak & Brew.

APRIL. Give him skin cancer, God, give him skin cancer, please!

DR. PEPPER. Excuse me, I know it's none of my business, but how long have you two been married?

APRIL. Three months.

ROY. And you were right the first time, it's none of your business.

APRIL. But we lived together a long time before we did.

ROY. Not long enough.

APRIL. Eight *centuries* it felt like!

ROY. Do you have to cry on the world's shoulder, April?

APRIL. I want us to work, Roy! I love you.

ROY. I know. I love you too, April.

APRIL. You're the best.

ROY. *We're* the best.

APRIL. You really think this Pepper fellow can help us?

DR. PEPPER. I'm no miracle worker.

ROY. You?

DR. PEPPER. Hi, Jason Pepper. Nice to see you.

ROY. You're Dr. Pepper?

DR. PEPPER. Let's make it Jason, shall we?

APRIL. Oh Roy!

ROY. The least you could've done was told us!

APRIL. I'm so ashamed!

ROY. Talk about seeing people at their worst!

DR. PEPPER. I'm used to that.

ROY. Yeah, but you haven't heard the other side of the story.

DR. PEPPER. And I'm sure it's a good one, too.

APRIL. Roy, I could just die. *(Hiram and Francis enter. They wear striped blazers, ascots, and white summer flannels. They cross to the table and will begin playing cards.)*

HIRAM. You know what they say about white flannels, don't you, Jason? The devil's invention. Never out of the cleaners.

FRANCIS. I put mine on first, of course, and then he decided he was going to wear his!

HIRAM. Don't be ridiculous.

FRANCIS. We *look* ridiculous.

DR. PEPPER. I think you both look rather dashing.

HIRAM. Thank you, Jason.

FRANCIS. Monkey see, monkey do.

DR. PEPPER. This is Mr. and Mrs. Pitt.

ROY. And you owe my wife an apology.

HIRAM. I don't recall speaking to you, Mac.

ROY. Now, look, you...

APRIL. It doesn't matter.

ROY. To me it does. You're my wife!

APRIL. Not in front of ... *(She motions toward Dr. Pepper.)* ... please?

HIRAM. Hiram Spane of the Newport Spanes, Mrs. Pitt. I've got a foul temper and a vicious tongue. Someone yells "ball" at me and they start working overtime. And that's about as much of an apology as you're going to get out of me.

APRIL. Thank you.

HIRAM. This is Francis Tear of the Baltimore Tears.

APRIL. Hi. April James, nice to see you. This is my husband, Roy.

ROY. *(Pumping Francis' hand.)* Hi, Roy Pitt. Nice to see you.

FRANCIS. Do you like to swim?

HIRAM. Francis!

FRANCIS. I just asked!

ROY. *(Gesturing for silence.)* Ssshh! Sshh! Sshh!

HIRAM. I beg your pardon?

ROY. Shut up! *(He listens, hears something.)* There it is! *(He and April cross their fingers.)*

ROY and APRIL. *(In unison.)* Baby, baby, baby! *(Roy runs off.)*

HIRAM. Is your husband mentally deranged, Mrs. Pitt?

APRIL. He's been expecting that call.

HIRAM. That wasn't my question.

APRIL. He's an actor. It might be a job. Normal people wouldn't understand. *(She sits.)* How long have you two been married?

FRANCIS. We're not married, Mrs. Pitt.

APRIL. Oh!

HIRAM. Oh?

APRIL. We have a lot of friends like that in the city.

HIRAM. Like what?

APRIL. Like you two. We're both in show business. We have to, practically.

HIRAM. Well, we're not in show business, Mrs. Pitt, and we certainly don't have to have friends like you.

APRIL. Did I say something wrong?

HIRAM. And I'm sure you're just getting started. Excuse me. *(He turns back to his card game.)*

APRIL. I was just trying to make small talk. I got better things to do than yak it up with a couple of aunties, you know!

HIRAM. I don't don't think normal therapy is going to work with that woman, Jason. Why don't you try euthanasia?

APRIL. Look, mouth!

DR. PEPPER. Children, children! *(Harry enters from the lake.)*

HARRY. Otto! Otto, pack my bags and put them in the car.

Just leave something out for me to change into. It's the black Volvo station wagon, the one with the snow tires. And then how about a round for everyone?

OTTO. *Jawohl Herr Scupp. (He goes.)*

HARRY. I'll be leaving right after lunch, Jason. I'm going home to take care of the kids. They need me. Dolly's decided to stay.

FRANCIS. Harry's leaving, Hiram!

HIRAM. I can see that, Francis.

DR. PEPPER. I haven't officially released you, Harry.

HARRY. I'm officially releasing myself. What were you planning on, Jason? Keeping me here 'til Doomsday?

DOLLY. *(Entering from the lake.)* Harry! Harry!

DR. PEPPER. What happened down by the lake?

HARRY. What didn't happen, you mean.

DOLLY. It was like our honeymoon.

HARRY. Don't make it sound too dramatic, Dolly. We just decided that our marriage was better than no marriage at all. I do what I want and she does what she wants. It's called compromise, honey, and it's the secret of a good marriage. If I want to fool around with someone you're going to let me because that's what I want to do and you want what I want. And if you want to fool around you won't because I don't want you to and you don't want what I don't want.

DOLLY. That's called compromise?

HARRY. That's called marriage.

DR. PEPPER. That's called *your* marriage.

DOLLY. That's called divorce.

DR. PEPPER. Just know what you want, Mrs. Scupp, not what you think you want. *(Dolly reaches for Harry's cigarette and takes a deep, satisfying drag.)* How is it?

DOLLY. Like honey. It's like someone just poured 10 years of honey down my throat.

DR. PEPPER. This is Mrs. Pitt. She and her husband have just arrived. They're on their honeymoon.

APRIL. Hi, April Pitt. Nice to see you.

DOLLY. Wait a minute! Wait a minute! The Crippled Children Telethon, right? That's her, honey. The girl we were so

51

crazy about. You sang "The Impossible Dream"!

APRIL. That was for Leukemia, actually, the Leukemia Telethon. For Crippled Children I did "Climb Every Mountain."

DOLLY. We think you're just terrific. You're headed straight for the top. I admire people like you so much. You're so selfless. *(Harry lets out a sudden, urgent scream.)*

DR. PEPPER. How was it, Harry?

HARRY. Fantastic.

DOLLY. Is he going to be doing that often?

DR. PEPPER. You might try it yourself sometime, Mrs. Scupp.

DOLLY. Me? I'm as cool as a cucumber.

DR. PEPPER. What brought that one on, Harry?

HARRY. The truth?

DR. PEPPER. You're still at Dunelawn.

HARRY. I want to *shtup* Mrs. Pitt.

DOLLY. Harry!

HARRY. You see how her tennis outfit's all slit up the side? There's no tan line. You know how women who are tan all over drive me crazy.

APRIL. What's the big deal? Your husband just said he wanted to *shtup* me. He didn't do it. *(Dolly lets out a sudden, urgent scream.)*

DR. PEPPER. How do you feel?

DOLLY. Hoarse.

HARRY. You'll get used to it. *(Roy returns. He is a changed man. April rushes to his side.)*

APRIL. Roy! Baby! Honey! What happened?

ROY. I didn't get it.

APRIL. Fuck them. What studio was it?

ROY. Fox.

APRIL. Fuck Fox. Fuck MGM. Fuck Disney.

ROY. They're going with Mel Gibson.

APRIL. And fuck Mel Gibson. He's this tall. He has to stand on a box to kiss someone.

DOLLY. I hope you're not the jealous type, Mr. Pitt. You're married to a very talented actress.

52

ROY. *(A shell of his former self.)* Hi, Roy Pitt, nice to see you.

APRIL. Roy's an actor, too.

DOLLY. Are you, dear? How nice.

HARRY. I knew I'd seen you someplace. That guy's not just a basket case, I said to myself, he's an actor! *(Explosively.)* The Elephant Man! You were in *The Elephant Man!*

ROY. *(A total relapse.)* The Elephant Man *(It's a terrible thing to see.)*

HARRY. What did I say?

APRIL. Nothing. You wouldn't understand. *(She will tend to him. Otto has returned with a tray of champagne. He passes it around. Everyone takes a glass. Harry turns to Hiram and Francis.)*

HARRY. I'm really going to miss you two guys. Take good care of her for me, will you?

HIRAM. When you come back for her, God knows we'll still be here. I think we're probably permanent.

FRANCIS. We're just lucky Hiram's mother can afford it.

HIRAM. No, you're just lucky Hiram's mother can afford it. So are you, Jason.

FRANCIS. Goodbye, Harry. I'll miss you.

DOLLY. No, no farewell toasts! This is a beginning. I want to propose a welcome toast to the new arrivals.

HARRY. You can't drink to yourself, honey.

DOLLY. All right, here's to new marriage and the Pitts!

HARRY. Here's to our old one, honey. It's gonna get better ('cause God knows, it couldn't get worse!)

HIRAM. Here's to real friendship.

FRANCIS. Here's to Hiram, the nicest thing that ever happened to me.

HIRAM. Why thank you, Francis. I take back almost everything I said.

ROY. Here's to April James.

APRIL. Here's to Roy Pitt.

FRANCIS. Who's April James, Hiram?

HIRAM. Some little RKO contract player, obviously.

DOLLY. Doctor?

DR. PEPPER. I feel I should make a long speech but I can see your arms are getting tired. Here's to ... happiness.

OTTO. Here's to Dunelawn. *(They drink. Then Harry starts to sing "Auld Lang Syne" and they all join in.* Much hugging, applauding and laughing.)* Lunch is served. The South Terrace in five minutes. *(They break apart and begin making their several exits.)*

FRANCIS. Will somebody just look at these flannels? Soiled already!

HIRAM. This time I'm sending your mother the bill. Old Bingo Money, that's all she is! Come on, Francis, let's get you tuned-up. We're playing through lunch.

FRANCIS. Can we play the Brahms G Major for Harry before he goes? Oh please, oh please! *(He will keep this up.)*

HIRAM. Oh all right, Francis, the Brahms G Major it is.

FRANCIS. I love the Brahms G Major. I'll set up. *(He rushes off.)*

HIRAM. He's like a child sometimes. I hope you like your chamber music mangled, Mrs. Scupp. *(He strolls off.)*

APRIL. *(Arm in arm with Roy.)* The people who cast those movies are the scum of the earth, honey. Never forget that. The scum of the earth. Say it with me: casting people are...

ROY. The scum of the earth.

APRIL. Again! *(They go.)*

ROY and APRIL. *(Off.)* Casting people are the scum of the earth.

DOLLY. I think we're doing the right thing, Harry.

HARRY. I know we are. Come on, let's eat. After lunch, she's all yours, doctor.

DOLLY. No, I'm afraid I'm all yours, Harry. *(Dolly and Harry walk off. He has his arm around her. There is a roll of thunder. Dr. Pepper looks up at the sky and feels his head.)*

OTTO. *Herr Doktor* does not want lunch today? *(Dr. Pepper shakes his head.)* *Herr Doktor* would like a martini? *(Dr. Pepper shakes his head.)* A little rubdown, maybe?

DR. PEPPER. *Herr Doktor* just wants everyone to be happy.

OTTO. Happy?

DR. PEPPER. *Du bist* happy, Otto?

OTTO. *Was ist* happy? *Wer ist* happy?

DR. PEPPER. A good question, Otto. *(Hiram and Francis are heard playing the Brahms G Major piano/violin sonata off. Dr. Pepper sits listening to it.)*

DR. PEPPER. I love it when they play together. It gives me hope.

OTTO. I'm going to cry.

DR. PEPPER. I don't think that was Brahms' intention, Otto. I think he wanted to give us something beautiful. That's enough. *(Otto goes. Dr. Pepper lifts his glass in a toast. Thunder and lightning. Dr. Pepper feels his skull. The guests are heard singing in the distance. Dr. Pepper sings along with them to himself, very quietly and slowly. His voice trails off. The curtain falls.)*

END OF THE PLAY

RAVENSWOOD

THE PLAYERS

RUTH BENSON, R.N.
BECKY HEDGES, R.N.
BRUNO
DR. TOYNBEE
MR. PONCE
MR. BLUM
MR. YAMADORO
HUGH GUMBS

RAVENSWOOD

*The setting is outdoors. The stage is bare except for a high
wall running the length of the rear stage wall. Also, there is
a small stone bench and scraggly tree. Nurse Benson strides
on. Nurse Hedges follows, pushing a medical cart.*

NURSE BENSON.   Hello. Ruth Benson, R.N., here. At ease.
Let's get one thing perfectly straight before we begin. I am your
friend. No matter what happens, I am your friend. So is Nurse
Hedges. *(Nurse Hedges smiles.)* But you know something? You
are your own best friend. Think that one over. I'll say the bell
tolls. It tolls for all of us. Welcome to Ravenswood. Shall we
begin? *(She claps her hands.)* Bruno! *(Bruno wheels in Mr. Ponce in
a wheel chair. Bruno is a horror, Mr. Ponce is a crabby old man.)*
Good morning, Bruno. Put him over there. Facing the sun!
That's right, Bruno. Thank you, Bruno. Now go and get Mr.
Blum.
BRUNO.   *(Looking/leering/lusting at Nurse Hedges.)* I'm supposed
to mow the lawn.
BENSON.   After you've brought everyone out here you can do
that.
BRUNO.   *(Still leering at Nurse Hedges.)* Dr. Toynbee says I'm
supposed to mow.
BENSON.   You can mow later, Bruno, mow all day.
BRUNO.   *(Taking a swig of whiskey from his hip flask.)* Mow and
trim the hedges. All the hedges need trimming, Dr. Toynbee
says. *(Provocatively, to Hedges.)* It's going to be a hot one. A
real scorcher all right.
BENSON.   Bruno!
BRUNO.   I'm going Benson, don't wet your pants. *(He turns
to go, then turns back to Hedges.)* Hey! *(Nurse Hedges looks at him.)*
Hubba hubba! *(He winks, leers, laughs, exits.)*
BENSON.   Ugh! *(Then, clapping her hands.)* Well, Mr. Ponce!
Good morning, Mr. Ponce! How are we feeling today?

MR. PONCE.   What do you think?

BENSON.   I think you're feeling one hundred per cent better, that's what I think!

MR. PONCE.   Who asked you?

BENSON.   Maybe you don't realize it, Mr. Ponce, but you are.

MR. PONCE.   I want a drink.

BENSON.   I didn't hear that.

PONCE.   I want a drink!

BENSON.   *(At a sound from Nurse Hedges.)* What is it, Hedges? You'll have to speak up, dear.

HEDGES.   Are we using serum?

BENSON.   Yes, serum! Of course, serum! *(The two nurses busy themselves at the medical cart during the following.)*

PONCE.   Liquor! Liquor! I want liquor!

BENSON.   Honestly, Becky, I don't know what's gotten into you lately.

HEDGES.   I'm sorry.

PONCE.   I want a drink, somebody!

BENSON.   You're sniveling again, Hedges.

HEDGES.   I am?

PONCE.   Will somebody get me a good stiff drink?

BENSON.   I'll cure you of that if it's the last thing I do.

HEDGES.   I don't mean to snivel. I don't want to snivel. I just do it I guess.

PONCE.   I need a drink. I must have a drink!

BENSON.   Well we'll soon put a stop to that.

HEDGES.   You're so good to me, Ruth!

BENSON.   I know. Syringe, please.

PONCE.   I don't want to stop! I like to drink! It's all a terrible mistake!

HEDGES.   *(Admiringly, while Benson prepares to administer the injection.)* No, I mean it. You're really interested in my welfare. I'm so used to women being catty and bitchy to one another, I can't believe I've found a friend who's deeply and truly concerned about me.

PONCE.   How much do you want, Benson? How much cold, hard cash?

BENSON.   It's called love, Becky.

60

HEDGES. I guess it is.

PONCE. Look at me, Benson, I'm making a cash offer.

BENSON. Good old-fashioned l-o-v-e.

HEDGES. Well I appreciate it.

PONCE. Where's Toynbee? Get me Toynbee!

BENSON. You're turning into a wonderful, warm, desirable woman, Hedges.

HEDGES. Thanks to you.

BENSON. Oh pooh! *(Mr. Ponce sees that she is about to stick him with the needle. He begins to yell and babble. He begins to jump up and down in the wheelchair as if he were strapped to it. His blanket falls off. He is! Also, he's wearing a straitjacket.)*

PONCE. Goddamn it, I want a drink and I want it now! I want a drink! I won't calm down until I get a drink! *(He's making quite a racket and carrying on like a wild caged beast. Benson stays in control. Hedges panics.)*

BENSON. Mr. Ponce! I'm not going to give you this injection as long as you keep that up. You're just wasting your time.

HEDGES. Do you want me to get help?

BENSON. I didn't hear that, Hedges.

HEDGES. I'm sorry.

BENSON. And don't start sniveling again.

HEDGES. So good to me!

BENSON. I'll have to report this to Dr. Toynbee, Mr. Ponce. I'm sorry, but my hands are tied. *(Dr. Toynbee strolls on. He has sad, benign eyes and a smile to match. Mr. Ponce immediately quiets down at the sight of him and hangs his head in shame.)* Good morning, Dr. Toynbee.

HEDGES. *(Almost a little curtsey.)* Good morning, Dr. Toynbee. *(Dr. Toynbee smiles, nods and looks at Mr. Ponce.)*

BENSON. Doctor, I think Mr. Ponce wants to leave Ravenswood.

PONCE. No!

BENSON. I don't think he deserves to be here. I'd say he's abused that privilege. *(Benson unfastens the straps that hold Ponce to the wheelchair.)*

PONCE. I'm sorry. I don't know what came over me.

BENSON. Get up.

PONCE. It was a temporary relapse, Doctor. I'm so ashamed, believe me, it won't happen again.

BENSON. *(Letting him out of the straitjacket.)* There's a long line of decent, honorable people waiting to get in here, Mr. Ponce. A very long line. And I think you'd better step right to the end of it. Well go ahead, you're free to leave now. I'm sure you'll be very welcome at that free-for-all across the lake.

PONCE. I can't look at you, Dr. Toynbee, I'm so ashamed.

BENSON. No one asked you to come here and no one's keeping you.

PONCE. Don't look at me like that, Dr. Toynbee!

BENSON. He said he wanted a drink. He demanded one, in fact. He even tried to bribe me, Doctor. *(Toynbee, his eyes never off Ponce, sadly shakes his head.)* Naturally I refused. So did Nurse Hedges.

HEDGES. *(Almost curtseying again.)* Yes, yes I did, Dr. Toynbee.

BENSON. Fortunately he revealed his true colors before I was able to administer the syringe. I'll have Bruno pack your things at once, Mr. Ponce. You'll find your statement in the checkout office. You won't be charged for today, of course. Now should they call your wife and family to come and get you or would you prefer the limousine service?

PONCE. Benson, wait, please!

BENSON. Dr. Toynbee is a very busy man, Mr. Ponce. Your wife and family or the limousine?

PONCE. I'm not leaving. I won't let you throw me out like this. You're sending me straight back to the gin mills if you kick me out of here. I'm not ready to leave yet. I'm not strong enough.

BENSON. Dr. Toynbee's heard all this, Mr. Ponce.

PONCE. *(Putting the straitjacket back on.)* Look, look, see how much I want to stay?

BENSON. Take that off, Mr. Ponce.

PONCE. *(To Hedges.)* Fasten me up, fasten me up!

HEDGES. Dr. Toynbee?

PONCE. The straps, the straps, just fasten the straps.

HEDGES. *(Moved.)* Poor Mr. Ponce.

BENSON. I wouldn't do that, Hedges.

HEDGES.　Dr. Toynbee? *(Toynbee, slowly, sadly, benignly, nods his head. Hedges buckles Mr. Ponce up in the straitjacket.)*

PONCE.　Thank you, Doctor, thank you! *(He would like to thank Dr. Toynbee, but now, of course, there is no way to do it.)* I'll be good, I'll be better! You'll see, you'll see! This will never happen again. Come on, Benson, you heard the doctor!

BENSON.　Surely, Doctor, you're not going to...? *(Again, Toynbee nods his head.)* That man is a saint.

PONCE.　God bless him.

BENSON.　Dr. Toynbee is a saint.

PONCE.　I am so grateful and so happy.

BENSON.　A saint!

PONCE.　I could kiss his hand for this. *(He tries to, and can't.)*

BENSON.　Should I proceed with the injection, Doctor? *(Dr. Toynbee smiles and nods.)* Hedges. *(Hedges helps her prepare another syringe as Dr. Toynbee moves to Mr. Ponce and stands directly behind him. He looks down at him, puts one hand on each shoulder and fixes him with a sad and solemn stare.)*

PONCE.　I can't bear it when you look at me like that. You're so good, Doctor, so good! I know how rotten I am. But someday I'll make you proud of me. I'll make me proud of me. I don't want to be me anymore. *(Dr. Toynbee smiles and bends down to Mr. Ponce's ear. When he does finally speak, it is totally unintelligible gibberish.)* You're so right, Doctor! Everything you say is so right! *(Toynbee turns to go.)* God bless you.

BENSON.　Thank you, Dr. Toynbee!

HEDGES.　Thank you, Dr. Toynbee!

BENSON.　Goodbye, Dr. Toynbee!

HEDGES.　Goodbye, Dr. Toynbee! *(Toynbee acknowledges them with a wave of the hand and strolls off.)* What a wonderful man he is.

BENSON.　That man is a saint.

HEDGES.　And so good.

BENSON.　Why can't we all be like him?

HEDGES.　How do you mean?

BENSON.　Perfect.

PONCE.　Please, Benson, hurry up.

HEDGES.　I think you're perfect, Ruth.

BENSON. You're sweet.

HEDGES. You are.

BENSON. Not really. And certainly not like Dr. Toynbee.

PONCE. Come on, Benson, before I get another attack.

BENSON. Do you realize he has absolutely no faults? Absolutely none.

HEDGES. No wonder he seems so good.

BENSON. He's perfect, Becky. I don't see why I can't get you to understand that. He has no place left to go.

PONCE. My hands, Benson, they're starting to shake!

BENSON. Dr. Toynbee wasn't born perfect. He worked on it and there he is.

HEDGES. You make it sound so easy.

BENSON. Take it from me, Becky, it isn't.

HEDGES. You're telling me.

BENSON. You're making wonderful progress.

PONCE. Oh my God, I'm starting to hallucinate.

HEDGES. Any progress I'm making is entirely thanks to you, I hope you know.

PONCE. A jeroboam of Bombay Gin!

HEDGES. I don't want to be perfect, Ruth, I know I never could be. Not like you.

BENSON. Oh pooh, Becky, just pooh!

PONCE. I'm salivating, Benson. Have you no mercy?

BENSON. Hang on there, Mr. Ponce, just hang on there another second.

PONCE. I'm going fast. I ... I ... I want a drink. I want a drink! *I want a drink!!! (Benson sticks him with the needle.)* I ... I ...

BENSON. Now what did you say you wanted, Mr. Ponce?

PONCE. *(A beatific smile spreading across his face.)* I don't want anything!

BENSON. Let's fix your chair now, so you get the sun.

PONCE. Yes, that would be nice, miss. Thank you, thank you.

BENSON. *(As she makes Ponce more comfortable.)* I pity your type, Mr. Ponce. Two martinis before dinner, wine with, a cordial after, and a couple of scotch on the rocks night caps. Social drinking, you call it. Rummies, I say, every last one of you.

PONCE. *(A long, contented sigh.)* Aaaaaaaaaaaah!

BENSON. All right now?

PONCE. I don't want anything. Any bad thing.

BENSON. Good for you.

PONCE. I'm going to make it, Benson. I'm going to be all right. *(His head falls over.)*

BENSON. Of course you are. And if you want anything, I'll be right over ... *(She takes his head and points it towards the medical cart.)* ... there. *(Benson tiptoes over to Hedges.)* Whew!

HEDGES. I admire you so much!

BENSON. Becky Hedges!

HEDGES. You can help me to get rid of my faults until you're blue in the face, but I'll never be the beauty you are.

BENSON. You're an adorable person, Becky.

HEDGES. I'm not talking about adorable. I'm talking about beauty. No one ever told Elizabeth Taylor she was adorable.

BENSON. Do I have to say it? Beauty is skin deep. Besides, Elizabeth has a lot of faults.

HEDGES. You're changing the subject. Ruth, look at me.

BENSON. Yes?

HEDGES. Now tell me this is a beautiful woman you see.

BENSON. What are you driving at, Becky?

HEDGES. Nothing. I just wish I were beautiful like you. And I don't want you to just *say* I am.

BENSON. I wouldn't do that to you.

HEDGES. Thank you.

BENSON. I said you were adorable.

HEDGES. And I said you were beautiful.

BENSON. It's out of my hands.

HEDGES. It's out of mine, too.

BENSON. You're sniveling again.

HEDGES. I know.

BENSON. *(She pulls Hedges over to the bench and sits her down.)* Becky, listen to me. You think I'm beautiful. Thank you. I can accept a compliment. But I wasn't so beautiful when I met and lost the love of my life, Hugh Gumbs.

HEDGES. Such a beautiful name!

65

BENSON. There you go again, Becky.

HEDGES. I didn't snivel that time.

BENSON. You made a stupid, flattering, self-serving, Minnie Mouse remark, which is much worse. Hugh Gumbs is not a beautiful name and you know it.

HEDGES. I'm sorry. I'll be good. I'll be better. Finish your story.

BENSON. I don't even remember where I was.

HEDGES. You were talking about your lack of beauty and how it cost you the love of your life, Hugh Gumbs.

BENSON. It drove Hugh away from me and into the arms of a beautiful hussy. He abandoned me for one Mildred Canby.

HEDGES. Mildred who?

BENSON. Mildred Canby.

HEDGES. What a horrible name, too.

BENSON. I know now what Hugh Gumbs wanted in a woman, what every man wants in any woman, is physical beauty and something deeper than beauty. He wants character. He wants the traditional virtues. He wants womanly warmth.

HEDGES. You can say that again.

BENSON. Believe me, Hugh Gumbs is a very unhappy man right now. How could he not be? Mildred Canby had even less character and more faults than I did. I knew that marriage wouldn't last. *(She takes out her compact.)*

HEDGES. Don't cry, Ruth.

BENSON. Me? Cry? Why should I cry?

HEDGES. Because you lost Hugh?

BENSON. I'm grateful to him! He broke my heart, I don't deny it, but if it hadn't been for Hugh I would never have been forced into the soul-searching and self-reevaluation that ended up with the 118-pound, trim-figured woman you say is so beautiful standing in front of you. No, when I think back on Ruth Benson then and compare her to Ruth Benson now, I thank my lucky stars for Hugh.

HEDGES. *(As Benson continues to gaze at herself in the compact mirror.)* You're so wise, Ruth.

BENSON. Am I?

HEDGES. Wise about love.

BENSON. I wonder.

HEDGES. You are.

BENSON. We'll see.

HEDGES. I'm not.

BENSON. *(Still distracted.)* Hmmmmmmm?

HEDGES. Wise about love. I'm downright dumb about it. If I weren't, I'd be married to Tim Taylor this very minute. What I wouldn't give for another chance at him!

BENSON. *(Regaining herself.)* Buck up, Hedges.

HEDGES. Oh I will, Ruth. I'm just feeling a little sorry for myself. I don't know why. If you want to know the truth, I haven't thought of Tim Taylor one way or the other for a long time.

BENSON. I should hope not. A man who smokes is a very bad emotional risk.

HEDGES. Tim didn't smoke.

BENSON. But he drank. It's the same thing. Rummies, every last one of them.

HEDGES. Did Hugh Gumbs drink?

BENSON. Among other things.

HEDGES. It must have been awful for you.

BENSON. It was heck. Sheer unadulterated heck.

HEDGES. That sounds funny.

BENSON. Believe me, it wasn't.

HEDGES. No, what you just said. About it being heck. I'm still used to people saying the other.

BENSON. It won't seem funny after a while. You'll see. *(Dr. Toynbee strolls across the stage, smiling benignly, reading a book.)* Good morning, Dr. Toynbee!

HEDGES. Good morning, Dr. Toynbee! *(To Benson.)* That man is so good, Ruth!

BENSON. I worship the ground he walks on.

HEDGES. Oh me, too, me, too! I'd give anything to be just like him.

BENSON. Goodbye, Dr. Toynbee! And thank you!

HEDGES. Goodbye, Dr. Toynbee! And thank you! *(Dr. Toynbee exits, waving.)* Ruth?

BENSON. What?

HEDGES. I know it's none of my business, but I've seen that look in your eyes whenever Dr. Toynbee passes.

BENSON. What look?

HEDGES. You know.

BENSON. The only look, as you put it, in my eyes when Dr. Toynbee passes is one of sheer and utter respect. Certainly not the look you're grossly alluding to. You're out of line, don't you think. Hedges? You're certainly in extremely bad taste.

HEDGES. You're not sweet on the good doctor?

BENSON. Dr. Toynbee is above that.

HEDGES. I know but are you? *(Benson slaps her.)* Is any woman? *(Benson slaps her again and they fall into each other's arms crying.)* I'm sorry, Ruth, I didn't mean to hurt you. You've been so good to me! I'm such a different person since I've been with you! I don't even know who I am anymore and I say these silly, dreadful, awful things! I don't recognize myself in the mirror in the morning. I've changed so much it scares me.

BENSON. You haven't changed. You've improved, refined, what was already there. I always had this figure, don't you see? Even when I weighed all that weight, I still had this figure.

HEDGES. Even when you were up to 230?

BENSON. I was never 230.

HEDGES. You told me you were...

BENSON. I was never 230! Now shut up listen, will you?

HEDGES. I'm sorry, Ruth.

BENSON. I didn't change anything. Mr. Ponce over there isn't changing. He's only emerging, with our help and Dr. Toynbee's into what he really and truly was in the first place: a non-drinker.

PONCE. A rum swizzle!

BENSON. People are born without any faults, they simply fall into bad habits along life's way. Nobody's trying to *change* anybody at Ravenswood, Becky. It's the real them coming out, that's all.

HEDGES. The real them!

BENSON. Look, face it, you've got big thighs, that's the real

68

you. Now I've got nice thighs, as it turns out, but I didn't always know that.

HEDGES. I don't think I can get any thinner.

BENSON. I'm not talking about diets. I'm talking about the real you and your G.D. big thighs!

HEDGES. That's exactly what Tim Taylor didn't like about me. And now that I'm getting thinner they look even bigger. I *know!* I'm sniveling again! I don't know what to do about them, Ruth! *(She is desperately hitting her thighs.)*

BENSON. Wear longer skirts!

HEDGES. Now you really are cross with me!

BENSON. You can be so dense sometimes. I mean really, Hedges, I'm talking about a whole other thing and you start sniveling about diets. You can diet all you want and you're still going to end up with big thighs. That's not the point.

HEDGES. What is it, then?

BENSON. Oh there's no point in talking to you about it!

HEDGES. I'm sorry.

BENSON. And stop that horrible sniveling!

HEDGES. I'm not going to get any better. I have just as many bad habits as when I came here. We just keep pretending I'm improving when the real truth is, I'm getting worse! *(She races to the medical cart and hysterically prepares one of the syringes.)*

BENSON. What are you doing?

HEDGES. Why shouldn't I? I'm no better than any one of them. I'm a disgrace to this uniform!

BENSON. Give me that! *(They struggle.)*

HEDGES. Let me do it, Ruth!

BENSON. Have you lost your mind?

HEDGES. I wish I was dead! *(Benson topples Hedges, who falls in a heap, and takes away the syringe. Almost without realizing, she reaches inside her blouse and takes a package of cigarettes out of her bosom, puts one in her mouth and strikes a match. Hedges raises her head at the sound.)* Ruth!

BENSON. *(Realizing what she has done.)* Oh my God! I wasn't thinking!

HEDGES. You of all people!

69

BENSON. I wasn't going to smoke one!

HEDGES. It's a full pack.

BENSON. It's a courtesy pack. In case I run into someone. They're not mine. I've given it up. I swear to God I have. You've got to believe me.

HEDGES. I don't know what to think.

BENSON. Becky, please!

HEDGES. If you say so, Ruth. *(Bruno enters pushing Mr. Blum in a wheelchair.)*

BENSON. It took you long enough!

BRUNO. I suppose it did. Where do you want her?

BENSON. *(Pointedly.)* Him. I want *him* over there. Facing the sun, next to Mr. Ponce. That's where I want *him*, Bruno. And then when you've put him there, I want you to bring out Mr. Yamadoro. And I want you to do it quickly this time.

BRUNO. I told you I was supposed to mow.

BENSON. We know, Bruno.

BRUNO. Mow and trim some hedges. Hey! *(He gives Hedges his hubba hubba leer.)*

BENSON. You're a beast, Bruno.

BRUNO. *(To Hedges.)* You got a light, baby?

HEDGES. No!

BRUNO. You, dog face?

BENSON. You know I don't. Matches and all other smoking paraphernalia are strictly forbidden here.

BRUNO. *(Taking out a hip flask.)* Yeah?

BENSON. So is alcohol.

BRUNO. No shit. *(Bruno downs a swig.)*

BENSON. The only reason Dr. Toynbee allows them to you is to set an example to the guests here. A bad example. On a human self-improvement ten scale, you rate about a minus fifty. You're a walking, sub-human nightmare, Bruno.

BRUNO. *(For Hedges' benefit.)* Sure is a hot one coming on. A real scorcher.

BENSON. Must you, Bruno?

BRUNO. Must I what?

BENSON. Stand there like that?

BRUNO. *(To Hedges.)* Now she doesn't like the way I stand.

BENSON. It's deliberately provocative.

BRUNO. What is that supposed to mean?

BENSON. Only you're about as provocative to a woman as a can full of worms. Now either get Mr. Yamadoro out here or I'll report you to Dr. Toynbee.

BRUNO. I'm going, Benson. Hold your bowels. (*He doesn't move. He is trying to think.*) What you said about a can full of worms ... I got desires. That's all I know, I got desires and I like to do 'em. (*He goes. Hedges curiously starts to follow. Benson claps her hands, and Hedges joins her.*)

BENSON. Good morning, Mr. Blum! How are we feeling today? Doesn't that sun feel good on you? And that delicious breeze from the ocean! And listen to those birds chirp! It's a day like this that makes you wish summer lasted all year! (*As she chatters away, she is preparing a syringe for Mr. Blum.*) When I was a little girl, we spent our summers in Vermont and my brothers and I used to go swimming in a little pond!

BLUM. Your cap, Benson. (*It's a gently desperate plea.*)

BENSON. Hmmmmmmm?

BLUM. Please. Just let me wear your cap. I won't hurt it. I'll just sit here and wear it. I won't say a word.

BENSON. Mr. Blum, I thought you were improving!

BLUM. I am, Benson, I swear to God I am! I just want to wear your cap for a little while. What's wrong with that? It doesn't mean anything. It's just a cap. I mean it's not like I asked to wear your skirt or your shoes or your stockings or anything! I'm all over that. A man could wear a cap like yours without it meaning anything.

BENSON. Does Dr. Toynbee know this?

BLUM. Are you crazy? Of course not!

BENSON. I'll have to tell him.

BLUM. It's not what you're thinking!

BENSON. We were all so proud of the progress you were making!

BLUM. As well you should be! I'm proud too! Benson, I haven't been in full drag in six weeks! You know what I was like when Martha brought me here. You've seen how I've

71

changed. You couldn't force me at gunpoint to put your shoes on.

BENSON. *(Immediately suspicious.)* My shoes?

BLUM. *Yes, your shoes!* Don't torment me like this! Your cap, Benson, it's all I'm asking for. Stop me before I want more.

BENSON. It's out of the question, Mr. Blum.

BLUM. I want that cap! I need that cap!

BENSON. Forget the cap! The cap is out!

BLUM. Five minutes, Benson, have a heart!

BENSON. Five minutes with the cap and next it will be the shoes and then the skirt and you'll be right back where you started. I know your kind, Mr. Blum.

BLUM. *(Bitterly.)* Do you, Benson?

BENSON. Give them a cap and they want your panty hose!

BLUM. What of it?

BENSON. You're here to change, not get worse! Think of your wife!

BLUM. What of her? I can't wear a size eight!

BENSON. Then think of your daughters.

BLUM. They're goddamn pygmies, too! I'm surrounded by stunted women.

BENSON. Do you know what they call people like you?

BLUM. Fashionable!

BENSON. You're a man, Mr. Blum, you were meant to dress like one!

BLUM. You're not God, Benson, don't you tell me how to dress!

BENSON. *(Holding back the syringe from him.)* I don't have to take that from you, Blum!

BLUM. What do you know about it?

BENSON. If you persist in defying me...!

BLUM. What does any woman know about it?

BENSON. Not only will I withhold this syringe...!

BLUM. Garter belts, Benson.

BENSON. I will fill out a report...!

BLUM. Merry widows!

BENSON. And give it to Dr. Toynbee!

BLUM. Black net stockings! Red garters, strapless tops!

Sequins!

BENSON. All right for you, Blum, all right for you! *(She starts out.)*

BLUM. Picture hats! That's right, Benson, you heard me, picture hats! *(Dr. Toynbee strolls on.)*

BENSON. Good morning, Dr. Toynbee.

HEDGES. Good morning, Dr. Toynbee! *(Dr. Toynbee smiles and nods.)*

BENSON. I want you to see something, Doctor.

BLUM. *(Head bowed, suddenly mortified.)* Please, Benson, don't. *(Benson begins to take off her cap. Blum watches in growing terror. Toynbee looks at Blum with such a great sadness.)* Benson, don't do this to me, not in front of him. Please. I beg of you. I'll change. I swear I'll change!

BENSON. He asked to wear my cap, Doctor. I think he should wear it. *(She puts the hat on his head. Blum writhes and twists in his straitjacket in the wheelchair as if he were on fire.)*

BLUM. No! No! Take it off! *(As Blum writhes and screams, Toynbee takes out his handkerchief and dabs at his eyes. Even Hedges cries.)*

BENSON. You've made Dr. Toynbee cry, Mr. Blum. I just hope you're pleased with yourself.

HEDGES. I can't watch, Ruth.

BENSON. *(Shielding her.)* It's all right, Becky, it's going to be all right.

HEDGES. To see the poor doctor cry!

BENSON. Sshh, sshh! Dr. Toynbee's here now. Everything will be all right. *(Dr. Toynbee slowly dries his eyes, puts away the handkerchief, and goes to Blum.)* Look Becky! *(Toynbee takes the cap off Blum. At once, Blum is silent and hangs his head. Toynbee stands looking down at him.)* That man is a saint. *(Toynbee hands the cap back to Benson, then turns and talks to Blum. Again, we can't understand his gibberish.)* Dr. Toynbee has that rare spiritual quality that when he just looks at you with those clear grey eyes of his you suddenly feel so ashamed of yourself you could just vomit.

HEDGES. Such a good man! *(Now Blum is the one who is crying. Toynbee asks for the syringe with a gesture. Benson gives it to him and he injects Blum. Benson wheels Blum next to Ponce, who is beginning to stir restlessly.)*

PONCE.   *(Very slurred.)* Bartender! I'll have a perfect Rob Roy on the rocks. I want a little service here, Bartender!

BENSON.   Doctor...? *(Toynbee smiles benignly and nods his head. He motions to Hedges that she should administer the shot.)*

HEDGES.   Me, Doctor...? *(Toynbee smiles at her and nods his head. Hedges approaches Ponce with a syringe.)*

PONCE.   Make it a double Dewar's on the rocks and hold the ice. *(Hedges looks to Toynbee for encouragement. He smiles and nods his head. She injects Ponce.)* Ouch!

BENSON.   *(Sharply.)* Hedges!

HEDGES.   He moved!

PONCE.   Goddamn mosquitos! *(Toynbee prevents Benson from helping Hedges out with a benign "let her do it" gesture. Hedges administers the syringe with no little difficulty. Ponce smiles blissfully.)*

HEDGES.   I did it, Ruth!

BENSON.   We saw you, Hedges.

HEDGES.   I really did it, all by myself! Doctor? *(Toynbee smiles and nods and begins to stroll off.)*

BENSON.   Thank you, Dr. Toynbee!

HEDGES.   Thank you, Dr. Toynbee!

BENSON.   Goodbye, Dr. Toynbee!

HEDGES.   Goodbye, Dr. Toynbee! *(Spinning herself around.)* Oh, Ruth, Ruth, Ruth!

BENSON.   Calm down, Hedges, it was only an injection.

HEDGES.   *(Still spinning.)* He's so tremendously, terrifically and terribly good!

BENSON.   You're not telling me anything about him I already didn't know. Now give me a hand here, will you?

HEDGES.   And you know something else? I'm a little sweet on the good doctor myself! *(She is still spinning and singing and dancing when Benson slaps her.)*

BENSON.   Snap out of it, Hedges!

HEDGES.   I'm sorry. You were right to do that. I'm not even worthy to mention his name. Who am I to think Dr. Toynbee even knows I'm alive? I'm dirt, Ruth. Next to him, I'm dirt.

BENSON.   Well...

74

HEDGES. Don't deny it. I know what I am. I've got big thighs and I'm dirt.

BENSON. You're too rough on yourself, Hedges.

HEDGES. I have to be if I'm ever going to get rid of my faults and be like you!

BENSON. I won't say "Don't aim too high, Becky" ... how could I? But I will say "Don't aim too high too soon."

HEDGES. *(Hugging her.)* Why are you so good to me? Everyone at Ravenswood is so good to me!

BENSON. Because we all love you and want to see you reach your full potential.

HEDGES. Zero defects.

BENSON. That's right, Becky, zero defects. No faults, no failing, no fantasy. It's a beautiful goal.

HEDGES. It sounds religious when you say it. With me it just sounds hopeless.

BENSON. Mark my words, Rebecca Hedges, R.N., the day you become perfect will be the most important day in your life.

HEDGES. It will?

BENSON. Mark my words. *(Bruno wheels in Mr. Yamadoro in a wheelchair. He, too, is strait jacketed and fastened down.)*

BRUNO. Okay, Benson, that's the Webster Hall lot. Where do you want him?

BENSON. Over there, Bruno.

BRUNO. Hey! *(Hedges looks at him.)* Hubba hubba!

BENSON. Thank you, Bruno. You can go now.

BRUNO. Who says I was talking to you?

BENSON. Aren't you supposed to mow now?

BRUNO. Maybe.

HEDGES. Mow and trim some hedges.

BENSON. Don't talk to that man.

BRUNO. That's right, pussycat. Mow and trim me some hedges.

BENSON. Then do it, Bruno.

BRUNO. Don't burst your bladder, Benson, I'm going. And don't think I ain't forgot that can of worms, horse-face.

BENSON. Bruno!

BRUNO. Stick around, kid. *(Hedges looks at him. He winks,*

leers.) Yes sir, a good hot day to trim me some hedges. *(He saunters off.)*

HEDGES.   The way he keeps saying that gives me the creeps. You'd think he meant me. *(She shudders.)* Jeepers creepers!

BENSON.   Good morning, Mr. Yamadoro.

HEDGES.   Ruth!

BENSON.   What?

HEDGES.   *(Referring to her charts.)* That's not Mr. Yamadoro...! *(Benson pushes her away from Mr. Yamadoro, furious.)* But it's not. It's Mr. Luparelli. Vincenzo Luparelli, Ithaca, New York. It says so right here.

BENSON.   He likes to be called Mr. Yamadoro. That's the reason he's here.

HEDGES.   I'm sorry. I forgot.

BENSON.   You forget everything! *(She turns back to Mr. Yamadoro.)* Good morning, Mr. Yamadoro, how are we feeling today? Any improvement?

MR. YAMADORO.   Much better, thank you, Nurse.

BENSON.   What about your urges?

YAMADORO.   You mean...? *(He lowers his eyes, blushes.)* ... I can't say it.

BENSON.   Yes or no? *(Yamadoro shakes his head "No.")* Isn't that wonderful! Did you hear that, Becky? Mr. Yamadoro feels he's improving!

HEDGES.   *(In all innocence.)* That's what they all say.

BENSON.   Watch your step, Hedges.

HEDGES.   Well, how come none of them ever seems to get any better? *(Benson slaps her and takes her aside.)*

BENSON.   Don't ever say that again! Don't ever even think it! *(Benson slaps Hedges.)*

HEDGES.   But they don't. *(Benson slaps her again.)*

BENSON.   *(She is shaking Hedges.)* Dr. Toynbee knows what he's doing. It's not his fault if his patients don't.

HEDGES.   I'm sorry. I just never looked at it like that.

BENSON.   Well maybe it's high time you did.

HEDGES.   *(Still being shaken.)* Now you're really, really cross with me!

BENSON.   A word against Dr. Toynbee and what he's trying

to do here is a slap in my face!

YAMADORO. Slap! *(He giggles.)*

BENSON. Now look what you've done. You've excited him. *(Indeed, Yamadoro has been vibrating with pleasure ever since this outbreak of violence of theirs. Benson goes to him, Hedges following.)* Now calm down, Mr. Yamadoro.

YAMADORO. You hit her. You hit her. Good for you, Benson, good for you!

BENSON. I didn't hit her, Mr. Yamadoro.

YAMADORO. You slap her then.

BENSON. No one slapped anyone.

YAMADORO. *(Calming down.)* They didn't?

BENSON. Did they, Nurse Hedges?

HEDGES. Oh no.

BENSON. What you saw may have looked like a slap but it wasn't.

HEDGES. Why would anyone want to slap me, Mr. Yamadoro?

BENSON. Sshh! You'll provoke him again!

YAMADORO. Impossible! It was nothing, nothing at all. A momentary relapse. My urges all are gone, my desires now like water.

BENSON. Pain, Mr. Yamadoro? You're not thinking about pain?

HEDGES. Ruth!

BENSON. I have to find out!

YAMADORO. Pain? There is no such thing.

BENSON. But in your fantasies? Come on, you can tell Benson.

YAMADORO. I'm all over that.

BENSON. Are you? Imagine, imagine Mr. Yamadoro, a beautiful, voluptuous woman ... blonde, why not? ... and she is at your mercy.

HEDGES. Ruth!

BENSON. I know what I'm doing!

YAMADORO. So far nothing.

BENSON. She looks at you, the tears streaming down her cheeks, the drug you've given her has begun to wear off, she's your prisoner and she can't escape. She sees your glowing slit eyes fixed on her fingernails. You want to pull them off, don't you, Mr. Yamadoro? One by one! *(Aside to Hedges.)* The fingernails, that's what they go for, these Jap sadists.

YAMADORO. *(Non-plussed.)* Continue.

BENSON. *(More and more graphically.)* Aaaaaiiiiiieeeeeee! She screams. Aaaaaiiiiieeeeee! Again and again! But you are implacable. Your cruelty knows no bounds. Your lust is insatiable. *(Angry aside to Hedges.)* Don't just stand there, Hedges, help me out!

HEDGES. Aaaaaiiiiieeeeee!

BENSON. But the room is sound-proofed and her bonds hold fast. Every exquisite torment the Oriental mind has devised you visit upon her helpless, quivering, palpable flesh.

HEDGES. Aaaaaiiiiieeeeee!

BENSON. There is no mercy, God is dead, and Satan reigns triumphant!

HEDGES. Aaaaaiiiiieeeeee!

BENSON. *(Savagely.)* Well, Mr. Yamadoro?

YAMADORO. *(Quietly.)* I feel a strange calmness over me. All human desires and passions spent. I desire nothing of the flesh.

BENSON. *(Triumphantly.)* You see?

HEDGES. He really does seem better.

YAMADORO. I really am, missy.

BENSON. Of course he is. *(They start to prepare a syringe.)*

YAMADORO. Dr. Toynbee is a saint.

BENSON. Back to work, Hedges.

YAMADORO. *(To Ponce and Blum.)* Don't tell Benson, but I just had an orgasm. *(He giggles.)*

BENSON. Can you manage this one yourself, too?

HEDGES. I think so.

BENSON. Good girl.

HEDGES. Thanks to you. *(Hedges moves in close to inject Yamadoro. He tries to bite her. She screams.)* Mr. Yamadoro, I thought we were all over that!

YAMADORO. It's never over! *(He is violent in the chair.)*

BENSON. Give me that. *(She takes the syringe, grabs him in an*

78

arm-lock, and injects him.) This'll hold him.

YAMADORO. (*A long moan.*) Mamma Mia! (*Benson and Hedges begin readjusting the wheelchairs. All three patients smile out seraphically.*)

BENSON. Look at them. Like babies now. It's a beautiful sight.

HEDGES. Everyone should take Dr. Toynbee's serum. Then the whole world would be perfect. No wars, no greed, no sex. No nothing. (*Bruno enters with a letter from the office.*)

BENSON. Mr. Ponce, Mr. Blum, and Mr. Yamadoro are going to be all right, Becky. It's only the Brunos of this world that are hopeless.

BRUNO. Hey, you in the white dress with the bird's legs!

HEDGES. I feel good just looking at them like this.

BRUNO. You want this, tight ass? (*He shows the letter.*)

BENSON. You're looking at the future, Becky.

HEDGES. In our lifetime?

BENSON. (*Sadly shaking her head.*) I'm afraid we're just the pioneers.

BRUNO. Hey, ugly-puss, I'm supposed to give you this.

HEDGES. A perfect world with perfect people.

BENSON. Someone has to do it.

BRUNO. There's a new patient, dog-face!

BENSON. Well, why didn't you just say so?

BRUNO. I did! (*Benson takes the papers from him, starts reading them over. Bruno exits, but not before a little "Hey!" and a few silent leers towards Hedges.*)

BENSON. Becky!

HEDGES. What is it, Ruth?

BENSON. I've been given another chance. Read this. I'm the luckiest woman alive. He's here. He's at Ravenswood. I've got him where I want him at last! Oh God!

HEDGES. Is it the same Hugh Gumbs?

BENSON. Do you know how many years I've waited for this moment? Hugh Gumbs wants to be a new person and I'll be the one helping him to mold his new self.

HEDGES. If I were you, I mean if this was Tim Taylor being admitted to Ravenswood, I wouldn't be standing here talking

79

about it. I'd fly to him.

BENSON. But... *(Indicating the patients.)*

HEDGES. Go on. I can take care of everything.

BENSON. You're a doll.

HEDGES. Now it's my turn: oh pooh!

BENSON. What am I waiting for? Wish me luck!

HEDGES. Luck! *(They kiss. Benson dashes off. Ponce, Blum, and Yamadoro are smiling. Hedges goes to the cart, gets a book, and crosses to the bench. Reading.)* A Critique of Pure Reason by Immanuel Kant. *(Bruno sticks his head up over the wall and whistles softly.)* "To Becky, with all my love, Ruth Benson, R.N." So good to me! *(Bruno whistles again. Hedges finally sees him.)* Please Bruno, I'm trying to concentrate. It's difficult material.

BRUNO. I thought we'd never ditch horse-face.

HEDGES. We?

BRUNO. It's just you and me now, Hedges.

HEDGES. I don't know what you're talking about.

BRUNO. I seen you.

HEDGES. Seen me what?

BRUNO. Looking at me.

HEDGES. I never looked at you.

BRUNO. I'm provocative. You heard Benson.

HEDGES. Provocative as a can full of worms is what she said.

BRUNO. *(Climbing down from the wall and approaching her.)* Only it ain't what she meant, is it now?

HEDGES. I'm not speaking to you, Bruno.

BRUNO. Benson looks at me, too.

HEDGES. Don't be ridiculous.

BRUNO. I seen her.

HEDGES. Ruth Benson wouldn't look at you if you were the last man on earth.

BRUNO. Around this place, that's exactly what I am. What do you say, Hedges?

HEDGES. You mean...?

BRUNO. I got a waterbed.

HEDGES. I don't care what you got. You're supposed to be mowing!

BRUNO. I'm done mowing.

80

HEDGES. Then trim some hedges! No, I didn't mean that. Stay back, Bruno. Don't come near me. I'll call Dr. Toynbee.

BRUNO. Toynbee looks at me, too.

HEDGES. Mr. Ponce! Mr. Ponce!

BRUNO. They all look at me,

HEDGES. *(Freeing Mr. Ponce from his chair and jacket.)* You've got to help me Mr. Ponce. He won't leave me alone. I'll get you a case of liquor if you help me!

PONCE. I'm on the wagon.

BRUNO. *(Exposing himself.)* Hubba, hubba, Hedges. *(Hedges screams and frees Mr. Blum.)*

HEDGES. Mr. Blum, I'll let you wear my cap or anything you want of mine if you'll just listen to me a minute. You don't understand.

BRUNO. *(Exposing himself again.)* Twenty-three skiddo! *(Hedges screams again, turns to Yamadoro and releases him, too.)*

HEDGES. Mr. Yamadoro, you've got to help me! You're the only one left. I'll let you hit me, if you'll just get up now.

YAMADORO. A strange inner peace has subdued the fires of my soul.

HEDGES. Oh shut up, you dumb Jap!

BRUNO. Your place or mine, toots? Let's go, sugar!

HEDGES. Help! Help! Help! *(She runs off. Bruno goes after her.)*

PONCE. We're free.

BLUM. I know.

YAMADORO. Yes, yes, yes, yes, yes.

PONCE. I don't want to leave, though.

BLUM. *(Draping the sleeve of his straitjacket around him like a boa.)* Neither do I.

YAMADORO. Celestial harmonies ring in my ears.

BLUM. What does that mean?

YAMADORO. I don't know.

PONCE. I once drank twelve extra-dry Gordon's gin martinis in the Monkey Bar at the Hotel Elysée.

BLUM. You should have seen me at the Beaux Arts Ball that time I took first prize. I went as Anouk Aimee.

YAMADORO. Exquisite woman.

BLUM. Yes, yes.

PONCE. Never heard of her.

YAMADORO. Wonderful fingernails. *(Hedges runs across, pursued by Bruno.)*

HEDGES. Bruno the gardener is going to ravish me and the three of you just sit there! Doesn't anybody care?

BRUNO. Hubba, hubba, Hedges! *(They are gone.)*

PONCE. I was so rotten when I was out there and over the wall.

BLUM. I could never find a pair of white heels that fit.

YAMADORO. Did I ever tell you gentlemen about Monique?

PONCE. I used to love to drink on Saturday. There's something about a Saturday.

BLUM. Do either of you realize what a really good dresser Nina Foch was?

YAMADORO. Monique was from Trenton. A lovely girl. *(Hedges enters and tiptoes to the house. Bruno suddenly appears from behind the hedge.)*

BRUNO. Hubba, hubba, Hedges! *(Hedges screams as they run out. We hear a "Help!" then the ripping of cloth.)*

PONCE. It's nice here.

BLUM. Peaceful.

YAMADORO. I desire nothing.

PONCE. Dr. Toynbee's serum.

BLUM. That man is a saint.

YAMADORO. Ravenswood is heaven on earth.

PONCE. I am so happy right now.

BLUM. We all are, Mr. Ponce.

YAMADORO. Life is beautiful.

PONCE. I can't stop smiling.

BLUM. And the sun smiles on us.

YAMADORO. And we smile back at it. *(He starts to sing, very softly — a World War I-type campaign song is suggested. Blum joins him. It becomes a duet in close harmony. Ponce just looks at them. When they finish, he speaks.)*

PONCE. I hate that song. *(Hedges appears.)*

HEDGES. What is it exactly that you want from me, Bruno? *(Bruno appearing, responds.)*

BRUNO. Hubba, hubba, Hedges!

HEDGES. You'll regret this, Bruno, believe me, you won't be happy! *(Hedges screams, and they both disappear.)*

PONCE. We really could leave now, you know.

BLUM. We'd just go back to what we were.

PONCE. You think so?

BLUM. I know.

YAMADORO. Oh, Monique! *(The three of them are really smiling now.)*

PONCE. A gin fizz with real New Orleans sloe gin. Disgusting.

BLUM. Fredericks of Hollywood. Revolting.

YAMADORO. Nina Foch spread-eagled. Hideous. *(This time it is Ponce who starts singing the song. The others join him for a short reprise as they each try to banish their private demons. They are just finishing when Benson wheels in Hugh Gumbs, still wearing his bedraggled street clothes.)*

HUGH. Aaaaaaaaaaaaaaaaaa!

BENSON. Mr. Gumbs, please!

HUGH. Aaaaa!

BENSON. You must try to control yourself.

HUGH. Aaaaaaaaaaaa!

BENSON. You're disturbing the others!

HUGH. Aaaaaaaaaaaa!

BENSON. It's obvious you're in great distress, Mr. Gumbs, but surely...

HUGH. I'm desperate, Nurse. You name it and I've got it, done it or used it.

BENSON. As soon as I've gone over your forms...

HUGH. Couldn't I just have my injection first?

BENSON. In a moment, Mr. Gumbs.

HUGH. I don't know if I can hold out.

BENSON. *(Keeping her head down, looking at her charts.)* Smoking. Three packs a day.

HUGH. That's right, Nurse.

BENSON. That's a lot, Mr. Gumbs.

HUGH. I'm not even being honest with you. It's closer to five.

BENSON.   Five packs?

HUGH.   Six, seven, I don't know! Some nights I set my alarm and wake up at fifteen minute intervals and have a cigarette.

BENSON.   Why?

HUGH.   Why? Because that's how much I like to smoke! What kind of question is that? Why? Why do people do anything? Because they like it! They like it!

BENSON.   Even when it's bad for them?

HUGH.   Yes! That's exactly why I'm here! I'm a liar. I'm a kleptomaniac. I chase women. I bite my nails. You've got to help me!

BENSON.   Thank God, Hugh, thank God!

HUGH.   What?

BENSON.   *(Back to the forms.)* A terrible drinking problem.

HUGH.   The worst.

BENSON.   How much exactly?

HUGH.   Bloody Mary's at breakfast, martinis before lunch...

BENSON.   How many?

HUGH.   Two, and three before dinner.

BENSON.   Wine with your meals?

HUGH.   No.

BENSON.   Well that's something.

HUGH.   Aquavit. And three or four cherry heerings after dinner and hot saki nightcaps.

BENSON.   It sounds like you still have your drinking problem all right.

HUGH.   Still?

BENSON.   *(Aside.)* Oh, Hugh, Hugh, you're breaking my heart!

HUGH.   Aaaaaaaaaaaaa!

BENSON.   I want to help you, Mr. Gumbs!

HUGH.   Then do it! Can't we all do this after the injection?

BENSON.   I'm afraid not.

HUGH.   *(Indicating the others.)* Look at them! How cured they seem!

BENSON.   You will be, too, Hugh. Excuse me, I meant Mr. Gumbs.

HUGH.   That's the first thing I'd like to change about me.

84

My name. How could any woman love a Hugh Gumbs?

BENSON. You mustn't torment yourself like that!

HUGH. I can't help it. I meet a woman and it's fine about the drinking, fine about the smoking, it's even fine about the ... never mind ... but when I tell them my name, it's all over. Ask yourself, nurse, would you want to go through life as Mrs. Hugh Gumbs?

BENSON. Surely there was one woman, somewhere in your life, who didn't mind your name?

HUGH. One, just one.

BENSON. You see?

HUGH. My mother, for Christ's sake! Please, can't I have my first injection?

BENSON. We're nearly done. A moment ago you said when you met a woman "it was fine about the smoking, fine about the drinking, it was even fine about the..." What's your "about the," Mr. Gumbs? Your worst habit.

HUGH. I can't tell you.

BENSON. I must have it, Mr. Gumbs.

HUGH. No.

BENSON. Your worst habit, I've got to have it.

HUGH. Believe me, you don't want it. *(Dr. Toynbee enters.)*

BENSON. This is Hugh Gumbs, Dr. Toynbee, a new patient. He won't tell me what his worst habit is. *(Dr. Toynbee goes to Hugh and stands, looking down at him with his hands on his shoulders, then bends and mumbles his unintelligible gibberish. Hugh bows his head, deeply ashamed, then motions Dr. Toynbee to lean forward while he whispers his worst habit into his ear, with much pantomiming. Dr. Toynbee straightens up, clearly appalled at what he has just heard, and leaves without even looking at Benson.)* In addition to all that, what really brings you to Ravenswood?

HUGH. I've told you.

BENSON. I thought perhaps there might be a somewhat more personal reason. I only meant perhaps someone else is responsible for your coming here.

HUGH. Like who?

BENSON. A woman.

HUGH. You're telling me! Say, and you're going to think

85

I'm crazy, did you ever work for an answering service?

BENSON.   No.

HUGH.   Your voice sounds so familiar.

BENSON.   I know.

HUGH.   There was this real battle-axe on my service about five years ago. For a minute, you sounded just like her. Where was I?

BENSON.   A woman.

HUGH.   Oh yeah, a woman. Yes, there is one.

BENSON.   Tell me about her.

HUGH.   *(With a sigh.)* She was very beautiful, very feminine, very desirable. Everything a man could want. Intelligent, decisive, yet strangely yielding.

BENSON.   *(Almost a murmur.)* Yet strangely yielding!

HUGH.   She's probably the finest woman alive on the face of this earth.

BENSON.   Her name, Mr. Gumbs?

HUGH.   House of Pork! Were you ever a hostess at the House of Pork over on 11th Avenue?

BENSON.   I'm afraid not.

HUGH.   You sound so familiar and I never forget a voice. Did you ever dispatch cabs?

BENSON.   No. Her name, Mr. Gumbs?

HUGH.   *(A tormented memory.)* Mildred Canby! Can I have my injection now?

BENSON.   What about Ruth Benson?

HUGH.   Ruth Benson?

BENSON.   I believe that's the name on your biography here.

HUGH.   I don't remember telling anyone about Ruth Benson.

BENSON.   You were delirious when they brought you in.

HUGH.   I was?

BENSON.   You were raving about a Ruth Benson. That's all you said. Ruth Benson. Ruth Benson. Over and over again.

HUGH.   What do you know?

BENSON.   She must have been very important to you.

HUGH.   Not particularly.

BENSON.   I'll be the judge of that. Tell me about her.

HUGH.   The main thing I could say about Ruth Benson is

that she was fat. About 280, I'd say.

BENSON. I'm sure she was never 280, Mr. Gumbs.

HUGH. You never saw Ruth Benson.

BENSON. 230 maybe, but not 280!

HUGH. The point is she was fat, right? I mean she was circus fat.

BENSON. I know the type. Go on, Mr. Gumbs.

HUGH. What else about her? I think Ruth Benson is the only person, man, woman or child, I ever asked to take a bath. Downwind of Ruth was a place you wouldn't want to be, nurse. She used to smoke six packs a day, minimum. Cigarillos. Nicotine stains right up to her elbows! I don't guess she ever drew a sober breath. My main image of her is passed out on the floor like a big rancid mountain. And talk about being a slob! She had dust balls under her bed the size of Volkwagens. She didn't just have roaches in her kitchen. She raised them. It was like a goddamn stud farm in there. You'd light the oven and there'd be a flash-fire from all the grease.

BENSON. It sounds like Ruth Benson was a woman with a lot of bad habits.

HUGH. She was an out and out pig.

BENSON. I can't help noticing a special glow that comes into your voice every time you mention her name.

HUGH. We had a lot in common, Ruthie and I. I'll never forget the night we each caught the other at precisely the same instant picking their nose. God, she was gross.

BENSON. There's that glow again.

HUGH. Just thinking of her with all those fingers up there and I have to smile. You're bringing back a lot of bad memories, Nurse. I haven't thought of Ruth Benson and her soiled sheets in a long time. Your voice sounds so familiar. *(Benson is making a big show of raising her skirt to fix a stocking.)* You have beautiful legs, Nurse.

BENSON. Familiar voice, unfamiliar legs.

HUGH. The legs look like some movie star, the voice still sounds like that answering service.

BENSON. *(Straightening up.)* Don't you know who I am yet, Hugh? No, don't say anything until I've finished. I'm not going to turn around until you tell me that you want me to turn around. I'm glad you don't recognize me. There's no reason that you should. I did it all for you, Hugh. Hugh Gumbs. Like your name, it wasn't easy. But I didn't mind the suffering, the self-humiliation, the incredible self-discipline. I wanted to torture myself into becoming someone a man like you could love and I have. Let me finish! I'm brutally honest with myself. That's not enough, I know, but it's a beginning. When I look in a mirror now I can say yes, yes, I like that person. I'm not smug, Hugh, I just know my own worth. For five years I've made myself thoroughly miserable so that today I could make you happy and I did it all for love. *(A pause.)* Now yes or no, Hugh, do you want me to turn around? *(A pause.)*

HUGH. Who are you?

BENSON. *(Turning to him, ecstatic.)* It's me. Ruth.

HUGH. Ruth?

BENSON. Ruth Benson.

HUGH. Fat Ruth Benson?

BENSON. Yes, yes!

HUGH. You don't look like Ruth.

BENSON. *(She is so happy.)* I know, I know!

HUGH. You don't sound like her, either.

BENSON. Voice lessons, darling.

HUGH. You don't even smell like Ruth.

BENSON. Zest, Dial, Dove, Lava!

HUGH. You have such beautiful legs.

BENSON. I worked for them.

HUGH. Your teeth.

BENSON. All caps.

HUGH. And your... *(He indicates her breasts.)*

BENSON. Exercises.

HUGH. Your big hairy mole.

BENSON. Cosmetic surgery.

HUGH. It's really you?

BENSON. It's really me. The real me and it's all for you, Hugh, I did it all for you.

HUGH. You did?

BENSON. And now that I've found you again I'm not

going to let you go this time.

HUGH. You didn't let me go the last time. I let you go.

BENSON. It doesn't matter. The point is you won't want to let me go this time. Oh Hugh, I'm going to make you very, very happy. You're the luckiest man alive.

HUGH. *(Shaking his head.)* No, Ruth, no.

BENSON. What's wrong?

HUGH. It would never work, Ruth.

BENSON. Of course it will work. It has to work.

HUGH. I couldn't do it to you.

BENSON. Yes, you can. You can do anything you want to me, don't you see?

HUGH. Ruth, I've committed myself to Ravenswood. They kicked me out of Dunelawn, I've gotten so bad.

BENSON. Do you love me?

HUGH. Love you?

BENSON. Be blunt with me, Hugh.

HUGH. I don't even recognize you, you're so terrific looking.

BENSON. Forget the way I look now and ask yourself: do you love me?

HUGH. You're so far above me now.

BENSON. From down there, do you love me?

HUGH. I didn't love you when you were fat and rotten. I can't love you now that you're beautiful and perfect and have such terrific legs.

BENSON. I'm not perfect.

HUGH. Well nearly.

BENSON. Nearly's not enough. Nearly's never enough. I still have my faults, too, darling.

HUGH. Like what? Name one.

BENSON. I can't off the top of my head but I'm sure I do somewhere.

HUGH. You see, it's hopeless. You're the sky above and I'm the mud below. Maybe someday I'll be worthy of you but right now I want to forget all about you and try to improve myself, too, and maybe, just maybe, you'll still be up there in the stratosphere, all shiny like an angel, when I poke my head up through the clouds.

BENSON.   That was poetic, Hugh.

HUGH.   And what does someone like me do with an angel?

BENSON.   Love her.

HUGH.   From a very great distance.

BENSON.   Where are you going?

HUGH.   I don't know.

BENSON.   I'm coming with you.

HUGH.   Angels fly. I've got to crawl first.

BENSON.   I'm not an angel. Forget the angel.

HUGH.   You're an angel!

BENSON.   I'm not an angel!

HUGH.   You're an angel!

BENSON.   I'm not an angel! It's the goddamn white uniform!

HUGH.   You're an angel. I can't even ask you for a cigarette.

BENSON.   Yes. Yes you can. Take the whole pack. I'll light it for you. You want a drink, darling, I'll get you a drink. Bruno! Go ahead, bite your nails. Do anything you want. I love you. *(She puts her fingers in her nose.)* It can be just like old times together!

HUGH.   Start that up again and I'll crack your jaw open! *(He pulls her hand away. Benson dissolves in tears.)* Oh, Ruthie, Ruthie! Don't you see how I'd drag you down? Trying to please me you'd only degrade yourself. Please, let's not talk about it anymore. Just give me the injection.

BENSON.   Then you don't love me?

HUGH.   I can't love you right now, you're just too darn good for me.

BENSON.   *(Fixing him with a new glance, all heavy-lidded and seductive.)* You think? *(She starts coming for him. She kisses him. A very long kiss. Hugh hardly responds.)*

HUGH.   Can I please have that injection now?

BENSON.   *(Her last resort.)* All right, Hugh, and remember, you asked for it.

HUGH.   *(Indicating the others.)* I just want to be like them. *(Looking at Yamadoro.)* Well not him maybe!

BENSON.   You will, Hugh, you will. *(Hedges and Bruno enter. Hedges' uniform is askew. She looks worn-out and dazed.)*

HEDGES. Ruth! Ruth! Ruth!

BENSON. Becky!

HEDGES. I'm turning in my cap, Ruth.

BENSON. Becky, what's wrong?

BRUNO. Hubba, hubba, Benson.

BENSON. What has he done to you?

HEDGES. Bruno and I are going to be married.

BENSON. What?

BRUNO. You heard her, mutt-face.

BENSON. What happened, Becky?

HEDGES. I'm in love, Ruth!

BENSON. What has the beast done to you?

HEDGES. Bruno's been saving up for a trailer. We're moving to Fort Lauderdale. Bruno's mommy has a pizza stand down there. This is goodbye, Ruth.

BENSON. *(Slaps her.)* Snap out of it, Hedges.

HEDGES. *(Finally, at long last and it's about time: snapping out of it and slapping her back.)* You snap out of it! That's all you do is slap people. *(She slaps her again.)* Only now you'll have to find someone else to slap!

YAMADORO. *(He is vaguely interested.)* Slap! *(Instead of doing anything, Hugh just sits there and pulls his coat over his head.)*

BENSON. All the time I've invested in you.

HEDGES. Are you ready, Bruno?

BENSON. You must be crazy.

HEDGES. I'm *happy!*

BENSON. I thought you cared about improving yourself.

HEDGES. Bruno likes me the way I am.

BENSON. He's a beast.

HEDGES. And I've got goddamn big thighs! Nobody's perfect!

BENSON. What about Ravenswood?

HEDGES. I won't miss it.

BENSON. What about Dr. Toynbee?

HEDGES. That man is a saint.

BENSON. Then why would you leave him?

HEDGES. He gives me the creeps.

BENSON. Zero defects, Becky?

HEDGES. *(Glowing.)* That's Bruno.

BRUNO. *(Triumphant.)* Hubba, hubba, Benson!

BENSON. Don't even speak to me!

BRUNO. Let's go, sugar.

HEDGES. *(She turns to Ponce, Blum and Yamadoro.)* If any of you had any sense, you'd come with us. There's enough room in Bruno's microbus for everyone. *(She fastens her cap on Mr. Blum's head, then turns to Hugh.)*

BENSON. Just go, you ... you pizza waitress!

HEDGES. Are you Hugh Gumbs?

HUGH. Yes, yes I am.

HEDGES. Are you in for it!

BRUNO. Hubba, hubba, dog-face!

HEDGES. Hubba, hubba, Ruth! *(They are gone.)*

BENSON. You'll regret this, Hedges, you'll regret this for the rest of your life! *(She turns to Hugh.)* Oh, Hugh, you see how terrible other people are! Thank God for Ravenswood and Dr. Toynbee. I'll get your injection right away. *(Hugh gets out of his wheelchair.)* Where are you going?

HUGH. I don't know! I can't stay here with you, Ruth. I'm not even worthy of Ravenswood. Maybe I'll come back to you one day, a better and worthier man. If not, I know you'll find someone good enough for you.

BENSON. It's a rotten world out there. It'll destroy you.

HUGH. It already has. *(He starts to go.)*

BENSON. *(Concealing the syringe.)* One last kiss. *(They kiss. Benson has the syringe in her hand, poised to inject him. Dr. Toynbee enters. Benson is mortified.)* Dr. Toynbee! I'm so ashamed. I ... Mr. Gumbs was just leaving.

HUGH. That woman is perfect! *(Hugh goes.)*

BENSON. I don't know what happened, Dr. Toynbee. I left them with Nurse Hedges and she's gone off to Florida to open a pizza stand with Bruno and the love of my life is gone again and I'm having a nervous breakdown because I don't understand people anymore. It's so good here. You're so good. Why would anyone want to leave Ravenswood when all we're trying to do is help them to be perfect? *(Benson is shattered. She is holding on to Dr. Toynbee for support. He puts his arm around her and takes her to the wheelchair left empty by Hugh Gumbs.)* You're so good, Dr. Toynbee. It's the end of summer. *(Dr. Toynbee goes to the cart to get a syringe.)* I won't cry. I refuse to cry. It's you and Ravenswood I'm thinking of. Not myself. The world is filled with men like Hugh Gumbs. But someone somewhere is the man for me. Zero defects. No faults, no failings, no fantasies. Where is he, Dr. Toynbee? *(She looks up into Dr. Toynbee's eyes as he injects her. A wonderful smile lights up her face.)* Oh, yes! *(Dr. Toynbee gets a straitjacket hidden behind the wheelchair and carefully puts Benson's arms through it. Meanwhile, Blum begins to sing again, very softly, the same World War I campaign song. Ponce, Yamadoro and even Benson join him. They are all smiling blissfully. In the distance, we hear even more voices beginning to sing. Dr. Toynbee smiles benignly at his three male patients. Then down at Nurse Benson. Then up at us. He starts to address us in his unintelligible gibberish, as a few leaves fall from the scraggly tree. The lights fade.)*

END OF THE PLAY

PROPERTY PLOT

DUNELAWN:

Portable cassette player (Otto)
Tennis rackets (Roy and April)
Luggage (Otto)
Martini glasses
Champagne glasses
Drinking glasses
Cigarettes
Matches
Book (Dolly)
Service bell (Pepper)
Orange juice container (Hiram)
Champagne bottle
Opera News magazine
Small box (Harry)
Ashtray (Harry)
Ukulele (Harry)
Tap board (Harry)
Ivory-tipped cane (Harry)
Drum set (Otto)
Purse (Dolly)
Mace cylinder (Dolly)
Tennis ball
Sun reflector (Rov)
Cocoa butter tin
Playing cards (Hiram)
Tray (Otto)

RAVENSWOOD:

Medical cart with supplies:
  bottles
  syringes
  other medical paraphernalia
Make-up compact (Benson)
Letter (Bruno)
Book (Toynbee)
Book (Hedges)
Hip flask (Bruno)
Medical charts (Benson)
Leaves

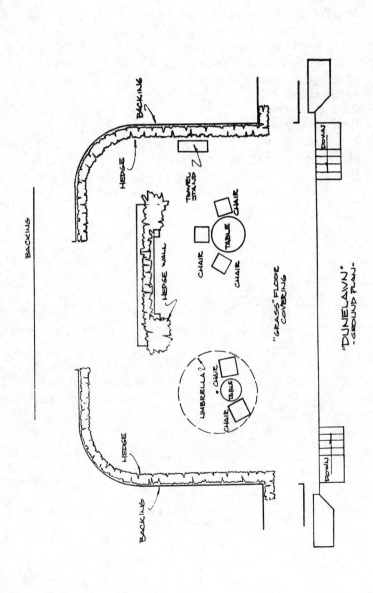

"DUNELAWN"
-GROUND PLAN-

BACKING

HEDGE

TREE

BOOKING

"BRICK" WALL

BENCH

HEDGE

BACKING

ENTRY

"GRASS" FLOOR
COVERING

DOWN

DOWN

"DUNELAWN"
- GROUND PLAN -

NEW PLAYS

★ MONTHS ON END by Craig Pospisil. In comic scenes, one for each month of the year, we follow the intertwined worlds of a circle of friends and family whose lives are poised between happiness and heartbreak. "...a triumph...these twelve vignettes all form crucial pieces in the eternal puzzle known as human relationships, an area in which the playwright displays an assured knowledge that spans deep sorrow to unbounded happiness." –*Ann Arbor News.* "...rings with emotional truth, humor...[an] endearing contemplation on love...entertaining and satisfying." –*Oakland Press.* [5M, 5W] ISBN: 0-8222-1892-5

★ GOOD THING by Jessica Goldberg. Brings us into the households of John and Nancy Roy, forty-something high-school guidance counselors whose marriage has been increasingly on the rocks and Dean and Mary, recent graduates struggling to make their way in life. "...a blend of gritty social drama, poetic humor and unsubtle existential contemplation..." –*Variety.* [3M, 3W] ISBN: 0-8222-1869-0

★ THE DEAD EYE BOY by Angus MacLachlan. Having fallen in love at their Narcotics Anonymous meeting, Billy and Shirley-Diane are striving to overcome the past together. But their relationship is complicated by the presence of Sorin, Shirley-Diane's fourteen-year-old son, a damaged reminder of her dark past. "...a grim, insightful portrait of an unmoored family..." –*NY Times.* "MacLachlan's play isn't for the squeamish, but then, tragic stories delivered at such an unrelenting fever pitch rarely are." –*Variety.* [1M, 1W, 1 boy] ISBN: 0-8222-1844-5

★ [SIC] by Melissa James Gibson. In adjacent apartments three young, ambitious neighbors come together to discuss, flirt, argue, share their dreams and plan their futures with unequal degrees of deep hopefulness and abject despair. "A work...concerned with the sound and power of language..." –*NY Times.* "...a wonderfully original take on urban friendship and the comedy of manners—a *Design for Living* for our times..." –*NY Observer.* [3M, 2W] ISBN: 0-8222-1872-0

★ LOOKING FOR NORMAL by Jane Anderson. Roy and Irma's twenty-five-year marriage is thrown into turmoil when Roy confesses that he is actually a woman trapped in a man's body, forcing the couple to wrestle with the meaning of their marriage and the delicate dynamics of family. "Jane Anderson's bittersweet transgender domestic comedy-drama ...is thoughtful and touching and full of wit and wisdom. A real audience pleaser." –*Hollywood Reporter.* [5M, 4W] ISBN: 0-8222-1857-7

★ ENDPAPERS by Thomas McCormack. The regal Joshua Maynard, the old and ailing head of a mid-sized, family-owned book-publishing house in New York City, must name a successor. One faction in the house backs a smart, "pragmatic" manager, the other faction a smart, "sensitive" editor and both factions fear what the other's man could do to this house— and to them. "If Kaufman and Hart had undertaken a comedy about the publishing business, they might have written *Endpapers*...a breathlessly fast, funny, and thoughtful comedy ...keeps you amused, guessing, and often surprised...profound in its empathy for the paradoxes of human nature." –*NY Magazine.* [7M, 4W] ISBN: 0-8222-1908-5

★ THE PAVILION by Craig Wright. By turns poetic and comic, romantic and philosophical, this play asks old lovers to face the consequences of difficult choices made long ago. "The script's greatest strength lies in the genuineness of its feeling." –*Houston Chronicle.* "Wright's perceptive, gently witty writing makes this familiar situation fresh and thoroughly involving." –*Philadelphia Inquirer.* [2M, 1W (flexible casting)] ISBN: 0-8222-1898-4

DRAMATISTS PLAY SERVICE, INC.
440 Park Avenue South, New York, NY 10016 212-683-8960 Fax 212-213-1539
postmaster@dramatists.com www.dramatists.com

NEW PLAYS

★ **BE AGGRESSIVE by Annie Weisman.** Vista Del Sol is paradise, sandy beaches, avocado-lined streets. But for seventeen-year-old cheerleader Laura, everything changes when her mother is killed in a car crash, and she embarks on a journey to the Spirit Institute of the South where she can learn "cheer" with Bible belt intensity. "...filled with lingual gymnastics...stylized rapid-fire dialogue..." –*Variety.* "...a new, exciting, and unique voice in the American theatre..." –*BackStage West.* [1M, 4W, extras] ISBN: 0-8222-1894-1

★ **FOUR by Christopher Shinn.** Four people struggle desperately to connect in this quiet, sophisticated, moving drama. "...smart, broken-hearted...Mr. Shinn has a precocious and forgiving sense of how power shifts in the game of sexual pursuit...He promises to be a playwright to reckon with..." –*NY Times.* "A voice emerges from an American place. It's got humor, sadness and a fresh and touching rhythm that tell of the loneliness and secrets of life...[a] poetic, haunting play." –*NY Post.* [3M, 1W] ISBN: 0-8222-1850-X

★ **WONDER OF THE WORLD by David Lindsay-Abaire.** A madcap picaresque involving Niagara Falls, a lonely tour-boat captain, a pair of bickering private detectives and a husband's dirty little secret. "Exceedingly whimsical and playfully wicked. Winning and genial. A top-drawer production." –*NY Times.* "Full frontal lunacy is on display. A most assuredly fresh and hilarious tragicomedy of marital discord run amok...absolutely hysterical..." –*Variety.* [3M, 4W (doubling)] ISBN: 0-8222-1863-1

★ **QED by Peter Parnell.** Nobel Prize-winning physicist and all-around genius Richard Feynman holds forth with captivating wit and wisdom in this fascinating biographical play that originally starred Alan Alda. "QED is a seductive mix of science, human affections, moral courage, and comic eccentricity. It reflects on, among other things, death, the absence of God, travel to an unexplored country, the pleasures of drumming, and the need to know and understand." –*NY Magazine.* "Its rhythms correspond to the way that people—even geniuses—approach and avoid highly emotional issues, and it portrays Feynman with affection and awe." –*The New Yorker.* [1M, 1W] ISBN: 0-8222-1924-7

★ **UNWRAP YOUR CANDY by Doug Wright.** Alternately chilling and hilarious, this deliciously macabre collection of four bedtime tales for adults is guaranteed to keep you awake for nights on end. "Engaging and intellectually satisfying...a treat to watch." –*NY Times.* "Fiendishly clever. Mordantly funny and chilling. Doug Wright teases, freezes and zaps us." –*Village Voice.* "Four bite-size plays that bite back." –*Variety.* [flexible casting] ISBN: 0-8222-1871-2

★ **FURTHER THAN THE FURTHEST THING by Zinnie Harris.** On a remote island in the middle of the Atlantic secrets are buried. When the outside world comes calling, the islanders find their world blown apart from the inside as well as beyond. "Harris winningly produces an intimate and poetic, as well as political, family saga." –*Independent (London).* "Harris' enthralling adventure of a play marks a departure from stale, well-furrowed theatrical terrain." –*Evening Standard (London).* [3M, 2W] ISBN: 0-8222-1874-7

★ **THE DESIGNATED MOURNER by Wallace Shawn.** The story of three people living in a country where what sort of books people like to read and how they choose to amuse themselves becomes both firmly personal and unexpectedly entangled with questions of survival. "This is a playwright who does not just tell you what it is like to be arrested at night by goons or to fall morally apart and become an aimless yet weirdly contented ghost yourself. He has the originality to make you feel it." –*Times (London).* "A fascinating play with beautiful passages of writing..." –*Variety.* [2M, 1W] ISBN: 0-8222-1848-8

DRAMATISTS PLAY SERVICE, INC.
440 Park Avenue South, New York, NY 10016 212-683-8960 Fax 212-213-1539
postmaster@dramatists.com www.dramatists.com

NEW PLAYS

★ **SHEL'S SHORTS by Shel Silverstein.** Lauded poet, songwriter and author of children's books, the incomparable Shel Silverstein's short plays are deeply infused with the same wicked sense of humor that made him famous. "...[a] childlike honesty and twisted sense of humor." –*Boston Herald.* "...terse dialogue and an absurdity laced with a tang of dread give [*Shel's Shorts*] more than a trace of Samuel Beckett's comic existentialism." –*Boston Phoenix.* [flexible casting] ISBN: 0-8222-1897-6

★ **AN ADULT EVENING OF SHEL SILVERSTEIN by Shel Silverstein.** Welcome to the darkly comic world of Shel Silverstein, a world where nothing is as it seems and where the most innocent conversation can turn menacing in an instant. These ten imaginative plays vary widely in content, but the style is unmistakable. "...[*An Adult Evening*] shows off Silverstein's virtuosic gift for wordplay...[and] sends the audience out...with a clear appreciation of human nature as perverse and laughable." –*NY Times.* [flexible casting] ISBN: 0-8222-1873-9

★ **WHERE'S MY MONEY? by John Patrick Shanley.** A caustic and sardonic vivisection of the institution of marriage, laced with the author's inimitable razor-sharp wit. "...Shanley's gift for acid-laced one-liners and emotionally tumescent exchanges is certainly potent..." –*Variety.* "...lively, smart, occasionally scary and rich in reverse wisdom." –*NY Times.* [3M, 3W] ISBN: 0-8222-1865-8

★ **A FEW STOUT INDIVIDUALS by John Guare.** A wonderfully screwy comedy-drama that figures Ulysses S. Grant in the throes of writing his memoirs, surrounded by a cast of fantastical characters, including the Emperor and Empress of Japan, the opera star Adelina Patti and Mark Twain. "Guare's smarts, passion and creativity skyrocket to awesome heights..." –*Star Ledger.* "...precisely the kind of good new play that you might call an everyday miracle...every minute of it is fresh and newly alive..." –*Village Voice.* [10M, 3W] ISBN: 0-8222-1907-7

★ **BREATH, BOOM by Kia Corthron.** A look at fourteen years in the life of Prix, a Bronx native, from her ruthless girl-gang leadership at sixteen through her coming to maturity at thirty. "...vivid world, believable and eye-opening, a place worthy of a dramatic visit, where no one would want to live but many have to." –*NY Times.* "...rich with humor, terse vernacular strength and gritty detail..." –*Variety.* [1M, 9W] ISBN: 0-8222-1849-6

★ **THE LATE HENRY MOSS by Sam Shepard.** Two antagonistic brothers, Ray and Earl, are brought together after their father, Henry Moss, is found dead in his seedy New Mexico home in this classic Shepard tale. "...His singular gift has been for building mysteries out of the ordinary ingredients of American family life..." –*NY Times.* "...rich moments ...Shepard finds gold." –*LA Times.* [7M, 1W] ISBN: 0-8222-1858-5

★ **THE CARPETBAGGER'S CHILDREN by Horton Foote.** One family's history spanning from the Civil War to WWII is recounted by three sisters in evocative, intertwining monologues. "...bittersweet music—[a] rhapsody of ambivalence...in its modest, garrulous way...theatrically daring." –*The New Yorker.* [3W] ISBN: 0-8222-1843-7

★ **THE NINA VARIATIONS by Steven Dietz.** In this funny, fierce and heartbreaking homage to *The Seagull*, Dietz puts Chekhov's star-crossed lovers in a room and doesn't let them out. "A perfect little jewel of a play..." –*Shepherdstown Chronicle.* "...a delightful revelation of a writer at play; and also an odd, haunting, moving theater piece of lingering beauty." –*Eastside Journal (Seattle).* [1M, 1W (flexible casting)] ISBN: 0-8222-1891-7

DRAMATISTS PLAY SERVICE, INC.
440 Park Avenue South, New York, NY 10016 212-683-8960 Fax 212-213-1539
postmaster@dramatists.com   www.dramatists.com